Portals

Portals

Two Lives Intertwined by Adoption

WILLIAM R. MILLER

and

LILLIAN KATHLEEN HOMER

Foreword by

GEORGE EMAN VAILLANT

RESOURCE *Publications* · Eugene, Oregon

PORTALS
Two Lives Intertwined by Adoption

Resource Publications
An Imprint of Wipf and Stock Publishers
199 W. 8th Ave., Suite 3
Eugene, OR 97401

www.wipfandstock.com

PAPERBACK ISBN: 978-1-5326-0444-7
HARDCOVER ISBN: 978-1-5326-0446-1
EBOOK ISBN: 978-1-5326-0445-4

Manufactured in the U.S.A.   10/05/16

To Dr. Rene Silleroy, companion on the journey—WRM

To my mother, Kathy Jackson, who has shown me
what a woman is supposed to be—LKH

Blessed are you who are hungry now, for you will be filled.

Blessed are you who weep now, for you will laugh.

—LUKE 6:21

Contents

CONTENTS

Foreword

PORTALS: TWO LIVES INTERTWINED *by Adoption* is the redemptive saga – opera really - of Bill (born in 1947) and Lillian (born in 1975). This jointly composed, riveting love story begins in 1947 when Bill comes into the world as part of the baby boom. His life is not without difficulty. At the University of New Mexico while becoming one of the world's wisest and most distinguished researchers in alcoholism, Bill and his wife realize that in order to have children they must adopt.

Few who knew Dr. William Miller ever called him anything but Bill. Nobody who knew Lillian ever called her Lil or Lilly. Together they decided to jointly tell in almost choral alternation a heartbreaking autobiographical story of twenty-four alternating chapters or really verses. Through more than three decades *Portals* illustrates how posttraumatic growth can occur. In contrast to Gounod's great opera, *Romeo and Juliet,* most of the chapters are filled with pain and heartbreak but *Portals* ends happily. After three decades of struggling attachment, Bill and Lillian remind me of another famous verse:

> Through many dangers, toils and snares I have already come,
> 'tis Grace has brought me safe thus far and Grace will lead me home.

Portals is Bill's and Lillian's joint effort to reassure themselves and the reader that at last they are safely home. Neither of them ignores the fact that God may have played a part.

Bill's and Lillian's joint story is one of courageous adaptation. Over and over again each suffered the pain of seemingly endless betrayal. Yet neither blames the blows that life inflicted on them; they only discuss how they adapted.

Bill's father's death occurred when Bill was a psychology intern. He tells us that at his father's funeral "On that day I felt the change from being one-who-is-cared-for into one who cares for others." That became his mantra for life. For Lillian, who was to become Bill's adopted daughter after social agencies removed her from her mother's neglect, the transformation came much earlier. "I can't really tell you why at such a young age I felt so mentally alert and grown-up but I guess it was just survival. I had to keep my brothers safe. It was my job to take care of them, or so I thought, which is quite a burden when you're six years old."

Portals is a harrowing tale. But it also is the story of Love. At the end of tumultuous decades together when Lillian at age forty leaves Albuquerque for Washington state, Bill writes, "We still stay in close touch, of course, through copious communication media, and yet I feel a dull ache within me as if something important is missing or incomplete. Of all the losses that come with aging this is a kindhearted one, arising not from want but from an abundance of loving."

Lillian, in turn, sings as she closes the book "I appreciate living more simply and having love and peace in my heart. How good life is!"

The reader is struck dumb, not having expected this love story to end any happier than Romeo and Juliet.

George Eman Vaillant, M.D.

Author and Professor of Psychiatry
Harvard Medical School

Authors' Preface

THERE WERE TWO MAIN reasons why I wanted to write this book. First of all I needed to. I thought that going back through my own story could help me and my family understand it better and come to peace with it. Writing it down has done that for me. I am definitely not proud of everything that happened or of some of the choices that I made. Yet this is what did happen and it brought me to the woman I am now. I thought hard about whether I really wanted to tell this very personal story to perfect strangers. A part of me just wanted to keep it secret, but I found that letting go of secrets can be healing in itself and this has helped me forgive those who hurt me.

The second reason is that I hope our story won't just be engaging but might be helpful and hopeful for others in understanding adoption or going through hard times themselves. Doctors told me that I had PTSD and I now think they were right, but people can be amazingly strong. Lots of kids have survived things way worse than what I went through. Your past doesn't have to rule your future. Maybe my story can help others discover their own strength as well.

Lillian

ADOPTION IS THE BEGINNING of a long and unforeseeable journey for both parents and children. Of course that is also true when having children of any kind. In considering adoption people often think of beginning with an infant but in fact the overwhelming majority of children in need of a stable home and family are between the ages of two and eighteen. Adopting older children is a unique experience because they enter the family not only with different genetics but with an extended period of separate and often traumatic life experience. By the time our own children came to live with us they had already experienced more trauma and suffering than any human being should have to endure in a lifetime.

During some of the darker periods my wife and I mused about writing a book entitled *Before You Adopt*. I am glad that we didn't write it then because it would have been incomplete, rather like asking a woman in the throes of painful childbirth for advice about whether to get pregnant. The years reflected in this book include some of the most difficult experiences of my life and I wouldn't have it any other way. I am clear that we did the right thing, what we were meant to do and be.

This is an unusual book for me. I have written for professionals and for public readers before but this is a book that I, like Lillian, needed to write. If it is engaging or useful for others we are pleased, but for both of us it has been a therapeutic working through of our experiences apart and together. We do not presume to advise anyone else on whether to choose adoption. We just tell our unfolding story.

This is also an interim story. Our lives remain a work in progress, an unfinished journey. One never knows where the road goes next. With Teilhard de Chardin, "I am content to walk right to the end along a road of which I am more and more certain, toward an horizon more and more shrouded in mist." It is enough.

Bill

1

Shamokin

Bill

AT LEAST AS FAR back as the sixteenth century both sides of my family lived in the Hesse region of central Germany. In fact their farms were only a dozen miles apart, so the families could even have known each other before the Müller ancestors immigrated to Philadelphia aboard the sailing ship Samuel of London in 1732. The Reitzes would arrive nineteen years later, also sailing into Philadelphia aboard the Duke of Bedford. Both families eventually settled in the Appalachian mountains of Pennsylvania.

My mother, Hazel, grew up in a now-razed three-story wood frame house at 103 West Sunbury Street in Shamokin. Her father, Bill Reitz, was a jovial fellow whose mother spoke a Pennsylvania Dutch blend of German and English, bequeathing to the family a colorful collection of sayings and stories. The town knew him as "Pappy" which was also his badge of honor at home. The Sunbury Street house in which I also grew up was on the main route through town for trucks hauling away anthracite coal from the Glen Burn Colliery just around the bend. We were located at third gear from the Market Street traffic light and day or night when trucks had to stop for the light they would be shifting up into third just as they passed our front porch.

The hill that rose directly behind our house is not nearly so high as I remembered but it seems far steeper now. I suppose it is the natural perspective of a boy that a hill looks like a mountain and each upward step is less daunting for shorter younger legs. We ran tirelessly up and down those slopes, exchanging volleys of rocks in games that now terrify me to recall as a parent. Mounted atop that thickly forested hill was another just as high, bare and black, formed of coal slag hauled up there from the mines in dump trucks winding their way up makeshift roads of hard packed culm. It was a forbidding, treeless place always leaching sulfuric smoke from the inextinguishable hell fires that burned deep within. We were forbidden ever to go up there, warned with tales of air holes, open maws that ventilated long-abandoned mine shafts far beneath. If a boy fell into one of those, as did one of my classmates, he was never seen again.

The footprint of our home was small, a twelve-foot-wide row-house design with narrow alleyways separating it from the Ference and Fiori houses on either side. Pappy had constructed the enclosed front porch from two glassed sound booths he had salvaged from a music store. Summer and winter we could sit out there watching the people and traffic pass by. At shift end the miners would file past, minstrel-faced with only their eyes showing where goggles had shielded them from the coal dust. Many of them would eventually die from black lung disease.

Behind the house was a narrow back yard with rosebushes and a grape arbor. A tree once stood there but had long since fallen into the earth in a mine collapse and been covered over. At the yard's end up against the mountain stood a grand two-story structure with peeling grey paint that we called the fish hatchery. It had been exactly that when the Reitz family operated a tropical fish store that later became Hazel's Gift Shop. After that Pappy turned it into a ramshackle carpentry shop where he puttered building and fixing things after he had retired from the Reading Railroad. From the second floor there was a back door that opened directly onto the hillside. More than once that old building shielded us from mudslides and flooding. I remember during one particularly heavy downpour watching torrents of coal slurry wash down the mountainside gushing jet black waterfalls over the neighbors' concrete retaining walls and into the basements of their homes on either side of us.

Bill Reitz was something of a folk hero in Shamokin. One midwinter night shift a buddy with epilepsy was working atop an icy boxcar when he suffered a grand mal seizure. In the post-depression era a laborer with epilepsy could lose his job if it came to the company's attention. With help from co-workers Pappy climbed up the access ladder and carried his friend down, caring for him until he came around. Bill married Lottie Savidge in 1911 and they had two children: my uncle Marvin and then my mother Hazel whose identical twin died at birth suffocated by the umbilical cord twisted around her neck. Lottie had an artistic eye and was the curator for the gift shop, which sold ceramics and novelties. She had a particular talent for handcrafting artificial flowers from colored wood fiber, a nearly lost art that she taught to her daughter. When Lottie contracted breast cancer she refused the recommended mastectomy. Instead Pappy drove her across the country to a chiropractic clinic in Denver that claimed to cure cancer, an extraordinary trip before interstate highways. The cancer metastasized and she died the following year.

Hazel graduated from Shamokin High School, but only her brother went on to college and became a music teacher. She worked in clothing mills—literal sweatshops—before I was born and again after I left for college. Her job title at one point was "turner," a person who turns collars, cuffs, and hems in an assembly line. She played piano and mandolin, loved jigsaw puzzles and games. She taught me to play chess as we sat under the grape arbor in summer. She had a child's playfulness, a simple rock-solid Christian faith, a love of stories, and undaunted optimism.

Ralph Miller, my father-to-be, was born in 1909 and grew up in Paxinos, a tiny rural village five miles from Shamokin. His father, Richard Miller, was a laborer for the Pennsylvania Railroad whom I remember as a lean, sullen fellow whose profile strikingly resembled the head of a Lincoln penny. Somewhere along the line he had committed some offense that was spoken of only in hushes, a sin that left him unwelcome in his own home. When I knew him after he had retired he would rise early in the morning and walk across Shamokin Creek on a railroad trestle to a garden plot where he composted and grew vegetables beside the tracks. He would remain there all day and this is where I would find him when we went to visit. We would sit together quietly, speaking occasionally but feeling no need of it. At dusk he would return for supper by kerosene lantern, where the table conversation flowed easily among my parents, Grandma Leah, my old-maid aunt Alda, and an affable if mysterious boarder named Lee. Grandpa Richard still said very little before retiring to his third-floor bedroom.

Leah was a more gregarious woman whose profile resembled the face of an Indian-head nickel. She tended a coal stove that doubled for cooking and winter heating. On its steel shelf she always kept a jar of Ritz crackers and a tin of warm ginger snaps or freshly baked soft molasses cookies. Without indoor plumbing there was a steel-handled pump outside that drew up iron-tasting water as well as a two-seater wooden outhouse, bitter cold in winter, provisioned with Sears catalogs. Inside the house was an earthen cellar that was cool year round where Leah stored her canned fruits and vegetables. There were stories—perhaps for my benefit, perhaps not—that this cellar was haunted.

Ralph left school after the eighth grade but did acquire a love of reading, particularly war novels. He met Hazel at a church weenie roast, a socializing precursor of the church potluck that centered on a bonfire over which, after it had settled down a bit, people would cook hot dogs skewered on sharpened branches while trying not to singe hands and face. Their courtship was interrupted by World War II when he was drafted and shipped to Fort Sam Houston in San Antonio to be trained as an Army baker. He never saw combat, however, and when he returned he went to work as a car inspector and yard laborer for the Reading line, one of the more fortunate men who worked above ground. They married in 1945, honeymooned at Washington D.C. and Hershey Park, and I joined the baby boom in 1947. Unable to afford a house of their own they moved in with the Reitzes, living up on the second floor. The tin-roofed third floor became my bedroom.

They were an unlikely couple, a blend of cultures. She was playful and happy, he fretting and serious, or so I remembered. In contrast to her anxious caution he rode motorcycles and liked guns. The Reitzes openly disapproved of Ralph and urged me, "Don't be like your father." In many ways I was not. He loved sports of all kinds; I was terrible at all of them and was most always picked late if not last for teams. He taught me to shoot and liked to hunt, but I wanted no part of it. I'm sure that in some ways I was a disappointment to him.

One of my earliest memories is of a game that we played. Down the center of the second story of the Sunbury Street house there was a narrow hallway. I remember my parents standing at one end of the hall and embracing. I would run down the hall and wriggle in between them, forming a snuggly kind of sandwich. It was a wonderfully warm and safe feeling. I remember Christmas seasons, too, that were filled with traditions. There was a large picture window facing Sunbury Street on the second floor as well as the front porch windows, and each advent Mom would draw Christmas scenes with chalk and then the family would fill in the pictures with tempura paints. Dad was in charge of putting bubble lights on the tree and then setting up the electric train and yard with figurines around it. It was well after Christmas before all of that was taken down and the windows were cleared – a day always tinged with sadness for my father.

Actually I have a still earlier memory that I recovered during a workshop on eidetic imagery when I was thirty-five. Akhter Ahsen had us imagine being at home as small children, looking at the furniture from a child's height. I had a very clear image of Pappy's living room, looking eye-level at the sofa cushions and chairs. Then just for a flash of a few seconds the scene changed and I was outside, looking up at a horrible face with blue sky behind, and a wave of terror swept through me. The face was pale white with wild red hair, and I remember the sensation that this figure was far too tall to be human. Then suddenly I was back in the safety of the living room again asking myself, "What the hell was *that*?" Thinking about it logically later it seemed like it might have been a clown with white face, stroobly (disheveled) red hair and a too-large grin. Would a clown perhaps have looked so terribly tall? I called my mother to ask whether she remembered me ever being frightened by a clown. "Oh yes," she replied, "I remember it well. We were on the boardwalk at Wildwood, New Jersey and you were in the stroller. A clown came along walking on stilts and tried to make you laugh, but you screamed, so he went away."

"How old was I?" I asked.

"You couldn't have been more than a year old," she said.

It wasn't until Sociology 101 in college that I learned our family was of low socioeconomic class. I had never felt poor. I had a few friends whose families were wealthy, but I don't recall any sense of envy or deprivation. There weren't many extras, but we were never hungry. At that time, one parent could support a family by working a full-time job.

Sometimes there comes an event that forever separates a family's history into before and after. My sister Frances, my only sibling, was born when I was five and quickly became the joyful apple of my father's eye. I loved being her big brother and I have many memories of playing together inside and out as she grew, teaching her to ride a bicycle and trick-or-treating at Halloween. I helped Pappy build an elaborate two-storey wooden dollhouse for her, complete with a staircase and furnishings. Once at the age of two she wandered out the alley door. My parents assumed that she had gone off with me on a walk (it was safe then for children to wander the city streets), but when I returned alone they realized that she was missing. We found her a few blocks away at the Picarelli family fruit market, perched happily on a stool and munching on an apple. At age five she was diagnosed with diabetes, and from there on she appears ever more pale and gaunt in family photos. At the age of eight she fell ill with infectious hepatitis on Good Friday and she died on Easter Sunday. There are no more 8 mm family movies after that. I vividly remember standing on our front porch raging, "Why God?" Yet I think that the tender wound of this loss opened in me a space for compassion.

2

Stockton

Lillian

MY NAME IS LILLIAN. Not Lil or Lilly, but Lillian. It's an old-fashioned name, and so is Viola which was my middle name. You don't meet many Lillians or Violas from my generation. I don't actually appear until chapter 4. This chapter is about my birth parents.

The story begins in Stockton, a city of about a quarter million people in the fertile San Joaquin Valley of California where grapes, nuts, vegetables and citrus are grown. Although Stockton is in central California it is also a seaport connected by the San Joaquin River to the San Francisco Bay.

My birth dad, Richard Calvin Zellner, was born in 1954 and had a pretty rough start in life. As far as he knew his birth parents had been good to him, but for reasons that he never understood they felt unable to take care of him even though they kept and raised his three sisters. What he remembered about his birth father was that he smoked a lot and could fill up an ashtray in half an hour.

Richard went into foster care at a young age, taken in by a police officer who had two older boys of his own. He told me that when he got into trouble his foster brothers would beat him. Tired of feeling pushed around, he often ran away and was in and out of various homes. Sometimes when he was as young as twelve he would live on the street because there he felt like he was on his own. I can't imagine how scary that would have been. It must have been really bad at his home if he felt safer on the streets.

Richard did not like school much. He was placed in special education which made him feel dumb so he would cut school whenever he could. He didn't think he belonged in the same class as the other kids there, even though his reading and math skills were pretty weak. At age fourteen he was introduced to heroin by a cousin and soon thereafter dropped out of school. At nineteen he was working as a beekeeper in Stockton, California when he met my birth mom through a cousin who had gone AWOL from the Army.

On my birth mom's side the story starts with her mother Carole, a wild and spunky lady who worked as a waitress in California and liked to go to bars and drink. With her first husband she had twin girls followed by another girl and a boy. I'm not sure why they got divorced, but soon after that she met my grandpa Wally, an alcoholic truck driver, and they lived in Alaska for fifteen years. They had two kids together, my uncle and then my mom Terry. Wally was abusive to grandma, though she could hold her own most of the time, and eventually they also divorced.

As the youngest child, Terry was often babysat by the twins who were the oldest so that grandma could work. The twins remembered her as being so fun and such a joy as a child. As a teenager, though, she started getting into trouble at school in Alaska and began using drugs. Terry was a tough kid because she had to be. She didn't get a lot of attention and had to grow up fast. Her sister told me that grandma gave the boys all the attention and liked them better than the girls.

When they moved back to California grandma met her third husband. They were together for a long time before they got married. Grandpa Lloyd really took in my mom and her brother like they were his own children. Grandma began to settle down and Lloyd tried to establish some discipline at home because my grandma never really did that. When he slapped or grounded Terry she would call the police and tell them that he abused her. Sometimes she ran away from home.

Terry was seventeen when she met Richard while partying in Stockton. They quickly fell for each other and were married soon afterward in 1974 at Lake Tahoe. Looking back, my birth dad told me they had been very much in love but were way too young to get married and raise children, not even knowing yet what they wanted in life.

3

Williamsport

Bill

HIGH SCHOOL HAD NOT been a particularly happy era for me. I was bookish and favored by teachers but felt like I had few friends. Before seventh grade we had been tested for academic ability and divided into home-room sections with sequential numbers that were a thinly veiled reflection of our expected aptitude. Our section 7-1 was the college-bound group, but the male paragon of that time and place was an athlete. Gym classes were dreaded humiliation and I lived with the adolescent sense that I ought to be something that I was not. I played trombone in bands and a disk jockey classmate let me help him spin 45 rpm records at high school dances, to which I attribute my partial hearing loss. Mostly I felt like I didn't fit. During my junior year death visited our family again when my beloved Pappy, aged seventy-six, died suddenly while driving on the way to visit his lover.

Somewhere in the course of childhood I experienced a calling to pastoral ministry. Having been baptized and raised Methodist I applied to the church-related Lycoming College in Williamsport Pennsylvania with the intention of going on to seminary afterward. It was, in fact, the only college to which I applied, so to make my application letter appear particularly neat and impressive I decided to fully justify the text so that the margins would be straight on both sides of the page. That's very easy now with a computer but on a manual typewriter it required calculating the number of extra spaces that had to be inserted in each line to make it right-flush with the rest of the text, then retyping the entire document while inserting line by line the requisite number of extra spaces in between words. I typed out a full draft and marked it up in pencil to calculate the spacing, then retyped the whole application letter on a new page. I sealed it up, addressed and stamped the envelope, and walked to the post office to mail it off. (This was long before photocopy machines.) When I arrived back home, sitting there on my desk was the perfect fully-justified version. I had mailed the marked-up draft! It was a portent of my life-long absent-minded professor inattention to detail. Horrified, I also mailed off the neat version in another envelope and hoped for the best. I was admitted anyhow, enrolling in the fall of 1965.

Arriving at Lycoming was like a homecoming for me. I discovered that I was on a campus full of people like me who loved the world of books and ideas. I lived with a roommate in the Wesley Hall dormitory. During that year I also kept in touch with a high school girlfriend, a pretty blonde who was going to Bloomsburg State Teacher's College. We decided to be married after my freshman year and lived off campus in Williamsport. In our first year together we rented a tiny studio next to the college, both working and surviving on a carefully-managed weekly budget.

I majored in psychology because it seemed like a good foundation for pastoral ministry and also in the vague hope of figuring out my own muddled head. My financial aid was as a research assistant to Dr. George Shortess, chair of the psychology department. His denizen included his office, several small rooms, an animal facility, and a large ramshackle work space in the basement of Bradley Hall. George (he had us call him that) was particularly interested in the physiology of vision in animals, and part of my job was cleaning out the rat cages, frog and turtle pens. We also built a Lashley jumping stand, a wooden structure with a platform facing two projection screens above water tanks so that a frog could choose to dive either to the right or the left. We projected patterns of lines onto the screens to determine which ones created more apparent movement on the frog retina—the sensation that closely spaced lines are moving. Frogs naturally jump away from movement when they see it, so I spent quite a few hours retrieving frogs from the water, replacing them on the diving platform, and recording which way they jumped when a new pair of patterns were projected.

There was a fad of turtle racing at the time whereby the competing turtles were simultaneously placed in the center of a large circle. The owners then backed away and the first turtle to meander across the perimeter was the winner. Since we had turtles in the lab I figured that a psychology student ought to be able to teach them how to run fast, but it turned out to be much more challenging than I thought. Turtles in a lab may only eat once a week, so popping little food treats was hopeless. Students at a neighboring college had tried electric shock to no avail. A twist of the tail only resulted in claustrophobic withdrawal into the shell. In a dusty corner of the work room was an old turntable abandoned by the college radio station, and in desperation I decided to see whether physical rotation might suggest the idea of motion to a turtle. I set the revolutions at 33⅓ per minute and placed one of our box turtles, Alice, on the turntable. Instantly she started scrambling for more stable shore; she apparently didn't like moving when she wasn't doing it herself. Here was something that turtles would work to avoid, and happily the way they avoided was to run. Soon Alice began running as soon as I put her down on the floor. If she failed to start running quickly I placed her back onto the turntable which launched her on her way. With this procedure she quickly learned to sprint a good ten to twelve feet in an impressively straight line. In her first official contest at Albright College, Alice crossed the outer perimeter in seconds winning fifty dollars. The runner-up, a dime-store turtle purchased that afternoon, finally wandered across the finish line several minutes later with most contestants still immobile.

At Lycoming I discovered that I could do some things I didn't even know were possible for me. Several professors gave me detailed feedback on papers, helping me learn to write. The Irish poet J. J. McAuley shared his contagious passion for finding just the right words to express oneself within the terse bounds of verse. I tried my hand as student conductor with the college band, directed a dreadful play, and worked as a teaching assistant for religion classes. I had never learned to swim but was required to do so in order to graduate. I particularly remember trying out for the college choir. In response to an open invitation from Professor Walter McIver three of us from his music appreciation class walked over to his office one day. I was nervous as he sat down at the grand piano keyboard, struck a note, and pointed at me. "Sing this pitch like this," he said, and I did. He stepped up the scale in half tones until my throat closed up and I said, "That's all I can do." "Oh my no," he replied. "There is much more there. I *like* what I hear. Did you know that you are a first tenor?" In the choir and voice coaching that followed, Walter McIver gave me a gift that would continue to bring me joy for the rest of my life.

I had been raised with a fairly simple fundamental childhood faith, and its foundations were definitely shaken as I learned about the multiple authors, contexts and inconsistencies of books of the bible. My parents, bless them, must have been distraught that I no longer believed biblical stories literally, but they always supported me to explore and discover and go my own way. I love Davie Napier's epigraph to *Come Sweet Death*, his dramatic cycle of poems on the Genesis stories: "These things never were but always are." By the time I was a senior I thought of myself as an agnostic. This troubled me and I went to talk to the campus chaplain about it. Instead of chastising me he told me "that's a good place to grow from." It was a few more years before I would reclaim my faith. In the meantime it didn't make much sense for me as an agnostic to go to seminary (although I later learned that this didn't stop others, particularly during the Vietnam War when seminary students were exempted from the draft), so I wound up applying to graduate schools in psychology. I didn't get into my first choice, the University of Oregon, so as a second-best I went to the University of Wisconsin which, little did I know, was one of the top-rated psychology departments in the country. But I'm getting ahead of the story.

I also learned that I could question authority. The President through most of my tenure at Lycoming had been Dr. Frederick Wertz. I remember him as a benevolent father figure who really fostered the atmosphere of excited and open inquiry that I found so appealing when I arrived on campus. What we discovered when he was called in 1968 to become a Methodist bishop was the extent to which he had served as a buffer between the board of directors and the faculty. Both groups liked him, and he was something of an insulating wall between them so that neither had much discourse with the other. That ended abruptly when the acting presidency was assumed by a board member, the CEO of Alcan Cable Company, who set out to remedy what he perceived to be serious problems on the campus. He produced a loyalty oath to the Methodist church that faculty would be required to sign in order to continue their contracts, but the act that crystallized opposition was his firing of the well-respected college dean who apparently could not get on board with the new agenda and style of governance. The effects were devastating. Over half of the faculty threatened to resign and at least a third did so that year. This led to one of the cleverest puns I've ever heard: "Alcany—the art of turning gold into lead."

My own involvement in this disturbing affair was as a concerned senior. I joined the editorial staff of *The Vacant Lot*, an underground newspaper mimeographed in secret and distributed by hand on campus. I was also one of four signers of a letter mailed in January to the homes of all students and alumni explaining the sequence of events and including statements of concern from eighteen faculty members. Correspondence flew back and forth with the acting president and was reprinted in *The Vacant Lot*, and I'm not proud of everything that I wrote then. Our public protests of the Vietnam War and of the changes on campus were quite timid in contrast to what was happening at large universities that year. We gathered on the steps of the library once to sing "We Shall Overcome" and wore black armbands at graduation, unaware that on both occasions Williamsport police cars were poised behind the library in anticipation of violence that never came.

I was twenty-one when I first tasted wine, that being the legal age for drinking. Beer was never appealing to me and I can't say that I much enjoyed the physical effects of alcohol which is mostly a depressant drug. It was also during college that I was introduced to marijuana. We became friends with a professional couple off campus who had easy access to high-quality weed. Never having smoked even tobacco I was intimidated when joints began to be passed around at parties. At first I just passed them on but eventually was persuaded to inhale. In friendly company it was relaxing, made jokes seem funnier, and definitely intensified food tastes. I can count on two hands the number of times I inhaled before leaving Williamsport.

I have said very little about my first wife. That is in part because I have so few specific memories. I surely knew very little about how to be a good husband to her. She married me with the expectation of becoming a minister's wife and that was not to be. I was engrossed in college, and while she socialized with students and faculty she was not pursuing her own education and was working to help us make ends meet. She was pretty and outgoing and I must have bored her, though I don't remember her ever saying so. This was the heyday of encounter groups and we went to several of those together where she was in her natural element as the very model of how people were supposed to be in that era: extraverted, emotionally expressive, spontaneous, ready and eager to try something new—all things that I was not.

It was around graduation that a faithful male friend broke the news to me that she had been having an affair with the man I regarded as my closest friend. The clues were everywhere but I had chosen not to see them and I must have been among the last to know. What I remember feeling is not anger but deep hurt and sadness. We were about to leave Williamsport which would accomplish geographic separation from her lover, so I forgave her and in a few days we were packing and headed for Madison, Wisconsin in the summer of Woodstock.

4

Manteca

Lillian

WHEN I WAS BORN in May of 1975 Terry and Richard had moved ten miles down the Central Valley from Stockton to Manteca, a much smaller California farming town. There seems to be something in our family that is attracted to small towns. Her father, Halbert Wallace, was born and raised in Norton, New Mexico, a spot so out of the way that it is classified by the census bureau simply as a "populated place."

Terry was eighteen years old when I was born and Richard was twenty. She told me that Richard introduced her to heroin some time that year and would shoot her up himself against her will, which is how she started using. Of course people don't remember much from their first year of life, but photos help create that memory for me. I have pictures of me in what looked like a normal family with that style of the 1960's, my mom wearing small tops and bell bottom jeans pulled up to her belly button. She would take me to parks to play on the slide and we had play groups with her friends who had babies, too. On my first birthday I had lots of presents and she said my favorite gift was a toy phone.

My brother Richard Halbert Zellner arrived twenty-nine days after my first birthday. He was just the cutest thing I had ever seen and I loved him so much. I liked playing with him and helping to take care of him. The four of us lived in a small apartment in Manteca. I don't recall much from this time, but it's funny what memories we do have from childhood. Some of them are very ordinary. I remember that Terry's father, our grandpa Wallace lived in an apartment with a round kitchen table that was green with gold edging and two green cushy chairs. He always had a bowl of sugar cubes on the table that I thought were candy. Some other memories from my childhood are terrible. One day the door opened and my birth dad came in covered with blood, saying that he had been shot. In our apartment there were stairs that came right down to the front door. Our telephone was on the stairs so he sat down there and called an ambulance. I don't remember the ambulance coming or anything else except seeing him lying there on the stairs with blood everywhere. I wondered for the longest time whether this memory was real or just a nightmare, but when I asked him about it he confirmed that it was true.

About a year after my brother was born we were living with some friends because times were hard. My birth dad told me a story that a little kid had knocked on our door and asked if we had any food because he was hungry. We had nothing to give the boy, and somehow this made our dad snap. He broke into a house and stole some food, was quickly caught and wound up spending three years in prison. Terry decided not to let him see or talk to my brother or me anymore and she divorced him. (Terry was usually a happy person, my birth dad told me, but when you got her mad "she sure had a temper on her.") It would be almost thirty years before I would see my birth dad again.

We left California and headed for Portales, New Mexico where grandpa Wallace had moved. The only way she could get there was to hitchhike. Don't ask me how I remember this since I was only two at the time, but for some reason I do. I remember walking along the freeway with my mom carrying Richard on one side and holding my hand on the other. She would put her thumb out and sometimes had me hold my thumb out, too. The only people who picked us up were truckers and they did not want to give her a ride for free if you know what I mean. She would pay them as she could with her body while Richard and I sat in the front seat. I remember thinking it was so cool to see all the gadgets they had in a big rig.

5

Heading West

Bill

MOVING TO WISCONSIN IN the summer of 1969 was the first time I had ever been west of the Pennsylvania border. Even Ohio had seemed so far out west that we couldn't imagine visiting our relatives there. I enrolled at the University of Wisconsin that summer to get a head start on my pre-doctoral training by completing two required statistics courses and an independent study, but that would quickly be interrupted.

The Vietnam War was at its peak and hundreds of thousands of young men were being drafted. The anti-war movement was strong in Madison and we got involved, joining in large street protests. We quickly met folks who were fond of marijuana and whose sexual exploits shocked my small-town sensibilities. In the process I discovered something important—that I was simply unable to perform the cognitive tasks required in graduate statistics if I had recently been smoking. That ended of my own experimentation with cannabis.

In 1969 the U.S. government implemented a new lottery system to determine randomly the order in which men would be called up for military service (something that is difficult for more recent generations to comprehend since the implementation of the all-volunteer army). Men were deferred from being drafted during college but that protection expired upon graduation. The draft lottery system went by birthdays, so one could receive a number anywhere from 1 to 365 depending on the drawing order. Men with birthdays on September 14 were the first to be called up that year. My number came up 64. In that first year of the draft lottery men with numbers up to 195 were conscripted—more than half of all men born between 1944 and 1950.

I had prepared for this possibility. In my antiwar involvement at Lycoming College I had contact with Quakers who were helping students apply for conscientious objector (CO) status. I had a clear pacifist history and the Quakers helped me prepare an application to my home draft board in Shamokin before the lottery numbers were drawn. It was a thick file including letters from veterans who disagreed with my stance but attested to my sincerity. I was later told that this was the first CO application my draft board had ever received. It was approved which meant that I was required to do two years of alternative service. To make it less convenient the government required that the service be performed at least 500 miles away from home, but because I was already farther away than that from Shamokin I was able to find a job in Madison working as a psychiatric aide, the lowest post on the staff totem pole. I took leave from the university and began work at Mendota State Hospital. There were other aides serving as COs there, and we got to do the grunt work of handling and restraining violent patients on locked wards. Mostly, though, we were the primary shift-long companions of people who were committed involuntarily for years or even decades. On our ward the patients were troubled teenage boys whose parents visited rarely if ever; visits that, if they did occur, usually left the boys even more agitated and disturbed than before. For my later career it proved useful to have started on the very bottom rung of the professional ladder and to have the opportunity of long hours in which to get to know those we were serving.

Just before Christmas my young wife told me that she wanted a divorce and left town with a fellow we had met in the anti-war movement. She asked for nothing—indeed we had almost nothing—and then she was gone. I don't blame her. We were so young, still sorting out who we were as individuals, and I had very little sense of what it takes to be a good life partner. That was a long cold winter. I first tried sharing the apartment rent with a roommate, an affable truck driver named Ed, then moved into the more affordable dormitory barracks at the mental hospital.

I still remember some of those lost boys on that adolescent ward and wonder what became of them. One gentle fellow had murdered his principal long before school shootings became a regular occurrence in the U.S. Some boys had explosive tempers or had run afoul of the law in other ways. Most, though, had just proved too "difficult to manage" for their parents and had been committed to the hospital indefinitely with the hope that they could somehow be repaired. This was the tail end of the era of mental hospitals as custodial warehouses. Soon psychiatric wards would begin emptying their patients onto the streets to become many of the homeless.

A woman whom I had been dating introduced me to a jazz pianist named Larry and we became fast friends. His day job was as a youth minister, though when we were out drinking he preferred to identify himself as a musician. When December of 1970 arrived he persuaded a university staffer who was a member of his church to host a Christmas party for young adults at the home she had been renting with two other women. Persuaded by Larry to come, I arrived with long hair and beard toting my acoustic guitar and settled into their downstairs fireplace room singing "Ain't Gonna Study War No More" and such. The stunning blonde hostess did not escape my attention and as I left I jotted down her home number from the round label on the wall phone's rotary dial.

Still licking my wounds from the divorce a year earlier I wasn't all that eager to commit to another relationship but I phoned her anyhow. Kathy Jackson turned out to be an Illinois farm girl who had recently completed her master's degree in student personnel administration and counseling. We seemed an unlikely couple—a university administrator and a street hippie—but I fell hard. To an introvert she was and still is astonishingly sociable as well as smart, kind, and funny with a large-hearted commitment to social justice. With her encouragement and Larry's I found my way back into the church and an adult faith. We sang together in the choir and began dating.

As my two years of service were drawing to a close in 1971 I was preparing to return to graduate school when I received a phone call from the director of clinical training telling me that there was a "problem" in the department. There had been an internal conflict between clinical and experimental psychology, he said, and half of the clinical faculty had already resigned including my advisor. There was no one particularly interested in my area of research, there would be no incoming students, none of the first-year classes that I needed would be offered, and financial aid was tenuous but I could still come back or he would help me be admitted elsewhere. I chose the latter option and ironically wound up being accepted to the University of Oregon, which had been my original first choice. Nothing had changed in my application except that this time I was applying from the University of Wisconsin with 40,000 students rather than Lycoming College with 1,200 students. It was enough to push me over the cut-off in their admission formula. I loaded all my worldly possessions into a 1970 Volkswagen beetle and headed still farther West.

I was truly clueless about graduate school, but again found that I loved it and could do well. Like most of my seven classmates I arrived with little inherent interest in doing research and intended to go into clinical practice, but over the course of four years all of us were trained to be clinical scientists and most of us wound up enjoying careers in research as well as clinical work.

Unsure of our relatively new relationship, Kathy and I were separated during my first year of graduate school. We kept in touch, though, by mailing cassette audiotapes back and forth. (Long distance phone calls were really expensive back then.) She came to Eugene to visit for Christmas that year. At church I had met a wise physician named John Bascom and his wife Ruth (later the Mayor of Eugene) who took me under their wing and treated me like part of their family. After meeting Kathy, John took me aside, put his arm around my shoulder and said sagely, "She'll wear well." How right he was. We were reunited and married in 1972 with wedding services in both Eugene and Madison, and we have been together ever since through the peaks and nadirs of life.

In the summer of 1973 we had the good fortune of a summer internship back in Wisconsin where I had my first experience with addiction treatment on an alcoholism unit at the Veterans Administration hospital in Milwaukee. Having the advantage of ignorance I practiced the listening skills that I had learned in my second year of training and spent the summer learning about alcoholism from patients on the unit. Although others would ask me later how I could possibly want to work with alcoholics I found that I loved talking with them. There was an immediate kind of chemistry for me, and understanding and treating addictions would become a core interest throughout my career.

In 1975 we moved to Palo Alto, California where I interned at the Veterans Administration hospital there. My first assignment was at the front door conducting intake interviews with people seeking mental health services. I would interview them, make a provisional diagnosis and refer them to appropriate service units in the hospital. It soon occurred to me that I could do this job for the rest of my life and never get any better at it because I never found out whether my diagnosis was correct or if they even arrived at the referred service: no feedback, no learning. This experience strengthened my interest in treatment outcome research which is what I had undertaken as my dissertation.

In September of that year my father died just as he reached the age for retirement. He succumbed to lung cancer even though he had worked above ground and had never smoked in his life. In his work for the railroad he had been exposed to asbestos and to the caustic spray chemicals used to clean out boxcars. The internship director lent us money to fly back to Reading for his funeral. On the cemetery lawn surrounded by friends and family we sat with my mother on folding chairs beneath a wind-blown canvas tarp suspended from four steel poles. He had run the race and completed his duty providing for his family, and my own work was just beginning. On that day I felt the inner change from being one-who-is-cared-for to one who cares for others.

Even at the beginning of internship I still had not decided what I wanted to do career-wise. The University of New Mexico that year was recruiting six faculty for the following fall and so began interviewing quite early in October. We flew to Albuquerque in November for my first job interview and I was offered an assistant professorship before Thanksgiving. It was "a bird in the hand" when nobody else was even interviewing, so we decided to go even though we knew almost nothing about New Mexico. As it turned out, we would never leave the land of enchantment.

6

Portales

Lillian

WHEN WE ARRIVED IN New Mexico we stayed with Terry's father for a while until he decided to move on to somewhere else. My mom did not want to move us kids again so she decided to stay there in Portales, a small town in dairy country near the Texas border.

A friend of grandpa Wallace said that we could live with her until Terry got back on her feet. During this time Terry got to know the friend's son and they started falling in love and eventually got married. It was a wonderful caring family who welcomed Richard and me as if we had been there all along. Our stepdad worked very hard to give us the lives he thought we deserved. In 1979 they had my little brother. He was sure cute and I thought he was mine.

After he was born, however, my parents' relationship grew more stressful. Terry started drinking a lot and we were not her priority anymore. That's when I became a caretaker. Every time they had a fight I took my two brothers into the bedroom that we shared. I always felt like it was my responsibility to be a mom to them. I tried to make sure they didn't get hurt or get into trouble which meant that they would get a beating. I hated to see my brothers hurt, so in order to protect them, most of the time I took the blame so they would not be beaten.

I'm not sure if Terry would have called it a beating; probably just "spanking," but she would drag me by my hair, slap my face, put cigarettes out on my legs and arms, kick me, spit on me and be very abusive verbally. There was always some reason for it: I would disobey or get into trouble somehow and then she would go way overboard on punishment. I always felt like I got the worst of it compared to my brothers. She told me that it was my job as the older sister to watch and protect them.

I know that Terry and my stepdad loved each other a lot at one point. They would often go out dancing. I'm not sure how old I was when my parents first asked a young man in his twenties to babysit us. When he came over we were hungry and I remember him trying to make eggs for us in the popcorn popper. He was fun and so nice to us. Later that night when my brothers were asleep he came and got me out of bed and told me that I could lie with him on the couch. I didn't fight or argue with him. I just did what I was told. He took all his clothes off, got under the blankets with me and rubbed my body with his, putting his hand under my pajamas. I just laid there and pretended I was asleep, afraid to say a word. Thank goodness my parents came home when they did because I am not sure how far he would have taken it. When he heard them coming up the drive-way he quickly got up and dressed and told me to go to bed and act like I was asleep or I would get into trouble. When my parents came in they were laughing and happy and asked why it smelled like burnt eggs. He explained about the popcorn popper and they all laughed. There were a few other times when I was at his house and if his wife wasn't home he would have me lie in bed with him and touch me until she got there, but he never hurt me. Till this day I still remember what his place looked like inside.

Terry tended to get particularly angry and mean when she drank. Twice she broke their car window, and I remember one day when she smashed all the dishes in the kitchen by throwing them on the floor. Often they would take us to friends' houses where they would drink. It was a crazy bunch of people. There was this one big guy we called Crazy Mike who always put his cigarettes out on his tongue. I remember one night when we were sitting outside with Crazy Mike and some other people drinking. My parents got in an argument and my stepdad decided to leave. He got into his car and Terry tried to stop him, punching him in the face through the open car window. He tried to drive away but she kept punching him, hanging onto the doorframe and eventually being dragged. There was a lot of blood. The next day everyone seemed fine as though it was just a normal night of drinking. My stepdad grew more sad and reserved over the rest of our time together. He worked long hours to keep food on the table and hated to leave us alone with Terry because he knew how she was.

I remember another time, maybe the last time they got into an argument, when Terry picked up a knife in the kitchen and ran around the house after our stepdad, screaming at him. We were hiding in the bedroom and our aunt came over and took us out of the house. She was always concerned about us and would do what she could to help us. She would bring us along on her errands or take us out to eat just to get us out of the house to where she knew we were safe for just that little time she had with us. She would sometimes come and clean us up and give us clean clothes to wear. I loved her for that.

Our stepdad couldn't take it anymore, and they got divorced after a year and a half of marriage. Things really took a turn for the worse at that point. Terry got a place of her own and I remember that she had a nice bed in the living room. My brothers and I had a room with two thin twin mattresses on the floor with no sheets, just comforters and nothing else. We had no toys. I remember always having to put my brothers to sleep when my mom would have parties and people came over, which was pretty much every night. Most nights we went to bed hungry and dirty. My brothers would cry and I would try to keep them quiet so my mom would not get mad, yell, and beat us. I remember hugging them close to me to stay warm and to protect them in case someone opened the door. I would stay awake as long as I could keep my eyes open. I don't think my mom meant to allow anyone to hurt us physically, but when she was drunk she never really cared or thought about the danger she put us in.

I can't really tell you why at such a young age I felt so mentally alert and grown up, but I guess it was just survival. I had to keep my brothers safe. It was my job to take care of them, or so I thought, which is quite a burden when you're six years old. I was really forced to take care of them, because if they were hurt or got in trouble I was the one who got punished. Crazy as it seems now, that's the way I wanted it. I would rather take the beating myself instead of my little brothers. When I look back on those experiences now I can still picture them in my head but it's a strange thing because I'm looking at me as if I was out of my body, seeing myself as a child in the picture.

Social services must have been called many times, but I don't remember them coming by to check on us. I do remember the one event that finally caused them to come and save us. This experience plays over and over in my head, almost like a guilty feeling. I'm not sure why I've carried that feeling with me into adulthood even though I know it wasn't my fault and I did the right thing.

My mom's boyfriend had us all over for dinner. I couldn't believe he had cooked liver and onions, which we thought was so gross. My brothers and I were eating very slowly and my mom told us we had to wait at the table until we finished our dinner. They went into his bedroom and although we were young we knew what was going on in there and I hated it. (I always hated it when she would have boyfriends. I felt like I had to protect her, too, because sometimes her boyfriends would hurt her.) I went over to the door to listen and giggle, then my brothers did, too. We took turns running to the door and then back to the table to act like we were still eating. Well, all of a sudden I heard this loud crash. I knew it must be the bed, so I knocked on the door and no one answered. I waited for a little while before I knocked again. My mom's boyfriend opened the door and he was dressed but where was she? I went in and looked for her and she was naked on the toilet. She screamed at me and told me to wait at the kitchen table. When she came out of the bedroom she was furious, though I don't really know why. She asked the man to spank my brothers while she spanked me. She beat me as she usually did with a belt. She had no control where it hit me—on my back, butt or my legs—because I always moved around. She would tell me, "Don't move or it will hurt." Really? It won't hurt if I don't move? The next day I could hardly walk but she sent me to school anyway.

At recess my friends were wondering what was wrong with me, so I showed them the bruises. The next thing I knew the physical education teacher (still to this day I remember what she looked like) came and took me to the office. Waiting there were the police and a lady from social services. They asked me who gave me the bruises and I didn't hesitate in telling them what had happened. I was just tired of being scared, though I was not aware of what could happen. They took me and my brothers away from my mom's home and we never returned there again.

We all went to the foster home of Mr. and Mrs. Jacobs who were very kind to us. Mr. Jacobs worked at the local newspaper and Mrs. Jacobs stayed home to take care of the kids. She was a good Catholic woman and I remember that she loved watching the TV program "M.A.S.H." They had a daughter named Lori who was my age, really smart and pretty.

On the day we arrived they gave us all showers and new clothes, putting all our old clothes in a black plastic trash bag because they smelled strongly of cigarette smoke. After that we went to bed and I remember hoping that my brothers would be there at the breakfast table because for the first time ever I did not sleep with them that night.

We weren't all there for long. My half brother got to go back to live with his father who had tried to take all three of us, but couldn't support us all financially. After a while they moved Richard to a different foster home, thinking it would be better for me so that I could be a kid and not feel responsible to take care of him. I didn't understand why they had separated us. I was mad, hurt and scared. It broke my heart not to have my brothers with me. I felt like my whole world was gone.

It didn't take long, however, for me to start relaxing and becoming a kid. Lori was a good friend and we played together a lot. She was never mean to me, though I did feel jealous of her at first because she got to eat at times when no one else did. It was because she had juvenile diabetes and had to have her blood checked all the time and then eat to get her blood sugar level right. Soon I realized that she didn't want it to be that way either. I loved being with the Jacobs and having a foster sister. We would play with Barbie dolls and dress up a lot. They had an attic with all these old clothes and we would play up there all day. The Jacobs had other foster kids but I couldn't even tell you their names now or what their own stories were. I don't even remember talking to them. In my mind it was just me and Lori. We would play together for hours at a time.

That summer the Jacobs bought a club house. Lori and I set it up the way we wanted. We put a table and dishes and a phone in there. I remember making mud pies and the Jacobs would pretend they were eating them. I have nothing but fond memories of these good people. Though they had other foster children to take care of, somehow they made me feel like I was the only one.

I was lucky to have stayed with the Jacobs for most of those two years. I don't know why but for some reason I did change foster homes once. When I arrived at Mr. and Mrs. Shaw's home my brother Richard was already there. He had already been with this family for a while. The Shaws were an older couple who had a note on the front door saying "Please do not ring the doorbell" because Mr. Shaw worked graveyard shift at the mill factory and so slept during the daytime. Richard and I shared a room. They put a cute stuffed animal on my bed and I was so excited to see my brother again and to be in the same room with him. It was like we had never been apart, though I did miss my good friend Lori. Mrs. Shaw was very strict but nice. If we put our elbows on the table she would take her fork and poke our arm. I only needed one reminder but I recall my brother getting forked often. We would roller skate a lot outside on the sidewalk so that we wouldn't make any noise inside. I wasn't there for very long. Soon I went back to the Jacobs and my brother stayed with the Shaws for a little longer. I am not sure why they moved me that time; I'm sure they had their reasons but didn't let the children know.

While we were in foster care we did visit our mom and step-dad every once in a while. There were times we would put on our Sunday best and get all ready for a visit and then Terry would not show up. I wasn't really surprised because I knew that drinking and drugging were more important to her, but it still would break my heart because these were the only times I got to see my brothers, too. One time we were able to spend a whole weekend with our stepdad. I was so excited that I would be seeing him, his mom and sister, and both of my brothers. Out of all the days when I could have gotten the chicken pox it had to be this very special day! I was not feeling well but I wasn't about to let anything stop me from going that weekend. I went to school and there was this bump that popped up on my stomach that I was scratching a lot. One of the teachers noticed and sent me to the nurse who then sent me home. I had a high fever and so couldn't go visit. They said that they would reschedule it for a different weekend, but that weekend never came. With the chicken pox I was really sick. I had a fever of 105 for days and Mrs. Jacobs would put me in cool baths and rub pink stuff on my pox which was a relief for a while. I would sleep a lot and had to be isolated until I was not contagious anymore. They didn't have a vaccine for chicken pox back then. In fact you wanted to get them when you were a kid because you could only get it one time and the sooner you got it over with the better.

7

Deciding

Bill

EVEN BEFORE WE CAME to New Mexico we had been discussing whether and when to have children. I had been part of a men's group during internship in Palo Alto, and beyond a few macho outings like white water rafting we met regularly to talk over personal issues at a time when it was not common to do so with male friends. My own ambivalence about having a family was high on my list of discussion topics.

During our first six years in Albuquerque much of my time and attention was focused on my university work and career, though we also became actively involved in a church. While I was absorbed in the achievement tasks of the first half of life the biological clock was ticking away on our childbearing years.

A sabbatical leave took us first to Norway in 1982 and then to Stanford University in 1983. Being back in Palo Alto I wanted to reconvene the men's group to catch up on what had been happening with everyone. We met at the home of some friends and I arrived early to visit with them and their children. Then the men arrived and we circled up, taking turns to fill each other in on the intervening years. When it came my turn I shared our continuing struggle about whether to have children. "Are you *still* stuck on that?" a friend despaired. So I explained how I just didn't feel any desire to have kids, and wasn't particularly fond of children.

The man sitting next to me erupted: "Bullshit!"

"What?"

"Bullshit! What were you doing when I got here tonight?"

"Well, I. . . was sitting down on the floor and playing with the children."

"Uh huh. And then what?"

"I tucked them in and read them a story?"

"Exactly. As a matter of fact, whenever I see you in a room with both children and adults, you're down on the floor with the kids. Now what's that about?" I didn't have an answer. It would not emerge until a few months later.

Now I need to say a bit more here about my father. My memories of him were of a silent, bitter, withdrawn man. I understand now that what I was seeing was clinical depression, which had probably plagued his father as well. He also had a bad temper. I don't think that he ever struck my mother but he did wallop me on occasion. There were some holes in the walls of our house where he had put his fist through when he got frustrated. He brooded about things and thought (quite justifiably) that life is not fair. He complained some, but mostly he just kept it to himself, and when he was quiet we knew enough to stay away from him.

Back home in Albuquerque after sabbatical Kathy and I were sitting on the couch having yet another conversation about having children when something peculiar happened. I suddenly began sobbing and for perhaps half an hour I found myself unable to speak. She just held me, and what happened was a downloading of memories of my father before my sister Frances had died. I remembered my dad playing with us on the floor, carrying us on his shoulders, holding us above the waves at the seashore, tickling us, playing hide-and-seek games and jumping out at us scaring us half to death. I remembered Decembers and how he loved to set up the electric train surrounded by a village of miniature buildings, people and animals underneath the Christmas tree. He spent a lot of time with us. He was a scoutmaster for years. He always wanted to teach me some kind of sport or outdoor activity, though I was never very interested in or good at those things. I did love stamp collecting, though, and he had a great collection, teaching me all about stamps. Later on he helped me build a train platform in my room.

What I realized in that painful epiphany was that I had also lost my father on the day that Frances died. He lived on for fourteen more years but was never the same. He loved her so much, and it must have been terrible for him to see her growing ever sicker over the years. His own religious background was Pentecostal, and during her final months he asked a faith healer to come by and pray over her. After she died the man came back to tell my parents that she had died because their faith was not strong enough—one of the cruelest acts I have ever witnessed. To my knowledge my father never accepted communion again, and for the rest of his life he remained depressed. Thank God my mother was more resilient, though she also bore a deep wound.

With the return of those memories I realized why I had sequestered my love of children, thinking "I want no part of anything that can do *that* to a man." I had continued to enjoy being with children while hiding and isolating it in my own awareness. What a remarkable puzzle is the human mind! I had shut away the pain until I was ready to deal with it. In that cathartic evening I was opened up to the experience of having children and before long we were trying.

8

Wednesday's Child

Lillian

I DON'T KNOW HOW many chances they gave my birth mom to keep us. Most likely they offered her some parenting classes and counseling and required drug tests. After we had been in foster care for about three years the authorities concluded that she was not going to change and terminated her parental rights. My half-brother could stay with his dad but the social workers decided that he couldn't support all three of us. They explored whether we might live with my Grandpa Zellner, but when they located him they discovered that he was recovering from a heart attack and unable to take care of us. When they tried unsuccessfully to locate my birth dad they decided that it would be best for us to be adopted. After posting the required notices in the appropriate newspapers his parental rights were also terminated.

At that time an Albuquerque television channel carried a weekly feature called Wednesday's Child. It was a way of letting people in New Mexico know about children who were available for adoption by telling some of their story during the evening newscast. Richard was eight and I was nine when a TV reporter told our story. I remember that she was really kind and helped us feel comfortable. She took us to Jerry's Perfect Pets in an Albuquerque mall where they did the filming. This mall seemed huge to us, being from a small town. I remember feeling shy, scared and happy all at the same time, and of course I was making sure that my brother was behaving himself. The news story began with us looking through the window at the dogs who were available for adoption and we each pointed to a dog we wanted to hold. I chose a big dog with long floppy ears while Richard chose a small fluffy dog to cuddle. The reporter made the connection for viewers that we were also waiting for someone to hold us. Playing in the background of the story was George Benson's recording of "The Greatest Love of All":

> I believe the children are our future.
> Teach them well and let them lead the way.
> Show them all the beauty they possess inside;
> Give them a sense of pride to make it easier.
> Let the children's laughter remind us how we used to be.
> Everybody is searching for a hero.
> People need someone to look up to.

As we held the puppies the reporter's voice-over said, "Lillian is a shy girl with a smile that can melt your heart. When not pouring out affection to a basset hound, Lillian is absorbed with her Barbie doll collection. Her brother is a bit more aggressive. The brightness behind his eyes tells you he knows what's going on all the time. His favorite activity is playing outdoors. The two want to be adopted together, so if you are interested in Lillian and Richard or any of our other Wednesday's children please call." She got it right, and the story aired a few days later.

We were not told, of course, how many people called, nor did we know how long it would take for someone to come along. We also did not know that the social workers had already been paging through a large book of information about potential parents who had already been approved to adopt, looking for a good match.

9

Twists and Turns

Bill

We attempted for two years to conceive, going through the phases of simply trying, then carefully timing, then undergoing diagnostic testing. When the next step became drugs or surgery we decided that there were plenty of children in the world who needed homes.

At the time we had to choose between fostering or adopting; parents were not allowed to adopt children they had been fostering, and so we opted for adoption. It took us more than a year to be approved. There were interviews with the Children, Youth and Families Division (CYFD) staff and social workers. They studied our home and our financial stability was scrutinized. We had thorough medical check-ups to make sure we were physically sound and our police and driving records were examined. We had to provide letters of recommendation regarding our character. None of these, of course, are required to become biological parents.

Finally we received notice that we had been approved. Infants were seldom available and yes, we would we consider older children who needed a home. Yes, we could consider taking two. Then we waited. And waited. Months passed.

After several calls to CYFD they dispatched a social worker to our home with a large book of children, an oversized family scrapbook binder. Each page showed the picture and told the story of a different child: age, gender, a bit of background, strengths and preferences, and what challenges he or she was likely to present. The turning of every leaf was a heartbreak. It was surreal to page through a catalog of potential children. "Just see if there are any you are interested in, and we can get you additional information." We felt no strong attractions, just a bit lost and overwhelmed. I remember there was one boy who had been in trouble for stealing money to buy books. We thought he had promise! Finally we said to get us more information about him and one of the few girls.

In paging through this book it struck me that such a large majority of children in need of homes are boys. By chance it should be half boys, but when a girl's home falls apart the extended family is likely to take her in. Perhaps troubled parents are also more reluctant to relinquish a girl. It is boys in particular who are left out in the cold. I felt and still feel a deep sadness about that fact. Boys get abandoned.

The next week we were sitting together watching the evening news, something that we rarely did. It was a Wednesday, and this channel included "Wednesday's Child." The reference is to a 19th century nursery rhyme that begins:

> Monday's child is fair of face.
> Tuesday's child is full of grace.
> Wednesday's child is full of woe.

The program featured children in need of adoption and on this particular evening the kindly reporter accompanied a brother and sister to a local pet store. They roamed the store holding dogs with Lillian beaming joy, Richard more reserved. "These children need someone to hold them, too" she said. Somehow in that moment we both knew that these were our children. Most people, had they been inspired by the show and telephoned, would have had little or no chance of adopting those children because of the year-long approval process, but we had already completed that screening and been cleared for takeoff.

So the next morning I telephoned the state office in Santa Fe, identified myself, and said we were interested in Lillian and

Richard. Instead of the delight that I anticipated there was silence on the line and then: "Oh, well. . . uh. . . we'll have to get back to you."

The wait this time was a few days. We asked friends to pray for us to have these children. Then we received a call to come in on Friday to meet with a team to "receive more information" about Lillian and Richard. When we went we learned the source of their hesitation. Over in Clovis, New Mexico, their social worker had gone through the book of potential parents and had picked us out. "Sorry," she had been told, "they are already interested in other children." Once that was cleared up at the meeting they gave us some documents as well as the picture books that Lillian and Richard had made about themselves and told us, "If you want them, they are yours." We were stunned. They wanted an answer about whether to proceed by Monday if possible, and we said yes.

We prepared a parent life book to be given to the children in advance with photos of ourselves, our home, and our cats. We wrote in it words of welcome and explained a bit about the kind of people we are. The try-out sequence was fairly straightforward. One weekend we would drive over to Clovis and spend a weekend with them in a motel with a pool. If that went well, the next week they would be brought to Albuquerque and spend the weekend in our home. If that went well the next week they could move in.

So we made the long drive across the high desert to Clovis and met with Margie, their social worker. After brief preparation a door opened and there they were in the flesh. "Hi mom! Hi dad!" Lillian exclaimed, giving us each a warm hug with Richard cautiously trailing behind her as we all headed off for the Holiday Inn. We spent time in the pool and hot tub and visited their favorite local eatery, the A&W root beer diner. The next day we drove to a public park, taking photos as they tried out the swings and monkey bars and posed among gnarled trees. We were all, I think, both excited and scared to be with these strangers who could soon become family.

On Friday of the following week there was a knock on our door. There they were with Margie and a change of clothes, pajamas, and supplies for the weekend. It didn't take long for a tour of our modest house. We had several meals together, went to a local amusement park, and attended church before Margie reappeared to take them back to Clovis.

And with that much information it was decision time, and we felt a big Yes. We drove over to Clovis to pick them up along with their few possessions. There was cake and a tearful goodbye party, the end of a long journey for staff and relatives alike. They moved in on Good Friday and the next day we went shopping for their new clothes for Easter. On Saturday evening they were baptized at the Easter Vigil service and on Easter morning, the very day my sister had died twenty-five years earlier, the streams of our lives flowed together.

10

Moving In

Lillian

I DON'T REALLY KNOW how many people were interested in adopting my brother and me. I didn't even know what the process was like to become adopted. That was not really what I was concerned about. I just wanted a family. I wanted a home.

Our social worker Margie was a very nice lady who made me feel comfortable. I remember her taking us on outings even when our birth mom was not available to visit us that day. I think she did that so we would feel wanted and so I could see and spend time with my brothers who were living in different places. We would go roller skating, driving around, visiting a park, and even just spend time at the state office where they had toys. Sometimes on these outings Margie would bring along her own daughter who was a lot older then we were and also very nice.

One day Margie came to get me from my foster home. We met my brothers at the social services office and that is where we got to meet a couple who were interested in taking Richard and me home. I felt like I already knew them because they had put together a photo album about themselves. It had pictures of them and the house we would soon be living in with their two cats Yin and Yang. I remember they had lots of rose bushes. There were pictures of our rooms—we we would each have our own room!—and in the album they told us that Bill liked hotdogs and music and Kathy liked making pies. It was such a good idea to make this book about them so we could see what kind of life they had. I loved all animals but had only ever had a dog named Bear. I remember feeling wanted and loved and so excited to be a part of the family. Even though we had not met them yet, it was the fact that someone was interested in us, someone could possibly want me and my brother and we could finally be together again. Margie also had Richard and me each make books about ourselves that had pictures of our birth family and of us as babies. Terry must have given those pictures to Margie. I still have those photo albums till this day.

After we met Bill and Kathy we ended up going to a hotel to spend more time with each other. It was such a nice hotel, and I think that was the first time we had ever stepped into a hotel room. We did things that kids like to do; we ate pizza, swam in the pool, and sat in the hot tub. I remember that my half-brother was there to swim with us. Looking back I think it was their way of saying that no matter what our half-brother would be part of our family as well. We had not seen him for a while and it was nice having him there with us, even though he was not going to be adopted.

The next day we went to a park at the sand dunes and played. I remember showing off my skills on the monkey bars, twirling over and over and then spinning on the merry-go-round. When it was time to say good bye I worried that we might never see them again. Maybe they wouldn't like us. So I just thought that we had a good time and that was that. Looking back I wasn't really expressing my emotions. When I cried I was beaten even more, so I had learned to be careful about showing how I felt, not realizing that I had programmed myself to have no emotions period.

Then the next weekend Margie took us to Albuquerque to stay in their house and again we did fun things that kids like to do. A week later it was time to move! We were so happy, our new parents were glad, and everyone we knew was happy for us. Even so I was also sad that I was leaving the only family I had known: some cousins, aunts and uncles I might never see again. There was a goodbye party for us at the social services office in Clovis, for which Richard and I dressed our best. We had cake and ice cream, and some family from my step-dad's side were there: my aunt, grandma, and the wife of one of my cousins with her baby girl.

When Richard and I moved to Albuquerque we were so happy to have a permanent place to live and to be together. I remember feeling relieved that this would be the last place where we would grow up and that we finally had a family to call our own. We called our adopted parents mom and dad right away. It was quite an adjustment for them, too, and they did well in making us feel right at home. My new father wrote a letter to Richard and me that I have always saved. He said:

> "This is a very special weekend for us all. We have wanted to have children for a very long time, and when we first saw you both on television in January, we knew in our hearts that we would all be together. Now it has really happened! You're here to stay and you can move into your very own rooms in your very own home, knowing that this time it's for good. We will love you and be your Mom and Dad while you grow up to become a woman and a man. In the years ahead there will be all kinds of times for us: lots of fun times, trips that we will take together, times of laughing, sometimes when we will cry, some quiet times, too. In all of this we can be together, always learning how to love each other. Welcome home!! We're so happy that you are here.

We were baptized in my parents' church on the weekend that we moved in and it was amazing. I had never been baptized before. My foster parents had been Catholic and so we were never allowed to take communion because we were not part of the church. My new parents' congregation accepted us as if we had been there all along. It really was a big thing. We each were given our own life candle and the ceremony seemed to be just for us. My parents were very involved in their church and we soon became involved too. Shortly after we moved in the people from church had a shower for us, like a baby shower but because Richard and I were not babies we called it an adoption shower. There were so many kind people there and I remember that it was both fun and exhausting. We got lots of fun gifts like games and clothes, which was nice because

Richard and I had almost nothing. I think that's when I began collecting stuffed animals.

As in our foster homes, our new parents had some rules to get used to, like we were only allowed one hour of TV on weekdays. Luckily there were other kids (mainly boys) on our road that we would do things with like make jump ramps for our bikes. That was mainly Richard's project; when I tried it I broke my tail bone! Our back-fence neighbors were pretty cool. I loved babies so I would go over there a lot to help her with their baby, or walk their German shepherds to the park. (That was scary sometimes because they wanted to get into fights with other dogs and I was too little to hold them back). We didn't lack for activities. Our new parents tried to get us involved in pretty much anything we were interested in doing. We were all trying to figure each other out. I'm sure it was harder on them in trying to work, figure out how to be parents for us, and deal with problems that Richard and I weren't even aware of, but in my eyes I was feeling more and more comfortable because it was a reality that this was my final place to stay.

In Albuquerque there is an amusement park called "Cliff's" where we liked to go. For fun my parents would sometimes tell us we were going to a surprise. They put paper bags on our heads with funny faces drawn on them and we tried to figure out where we were going from turns and sounds. It wasn't very far, but dad drove all around to disguise where we were going. There are so many fun memories I have with my adopted parents. Mom took us shopping and we did lots of things with friends. We would have game night once a week, and every Sunday we watched a TV show together that we liked and had peanut butter and jelly sandwiches with popcorn. (Actually mom had peanut butter and onion sandwiches, a tradition from her family, but we stuck with jelly.)

On my birthday that year I was turning 10 and since I had been at school I already had made some pretty good friends. My parents set up this awesome party and I remember dad having set up a wooden plank. We were blindfolded and we would get on this plank and he would move it while we laughed and screamed. We also had apples hanging from the clothesline which was fun too. I had never had a birthday party like this but I was quickly getting used to a new social life. My parents did everything they could to help us feel comfortable and find things for us to do. We also got into counseling and family therapy to talk about what we had been through earlier in life.

In that first year we met more of our new family. Mom is the oldest of seven kids so we met plenty of new uncles, aunts and cousins and got along with them really well. We went by train to visit them in Illinois which was fun and they all accepted us immediately as part of the family. Mom's sister also had two kids who were adopted so we were not the only ones who were not born into the family. My mom's mother, my grandma Jackson was a little on the strict side but we loved her and if she was alive today I would like to sit down with her and ask her some questions.

My dad's mother was a funny and happy lady, always smiling. I remember that her favorite saying was from a reggae song, "Don't worry be happy," and she had a sweatshirt with those words and a bright yellow smiley face. One year when my parents went to Russia for two weeks grandma Miller was brave enough to have us live with her at her mobile home in Reading, Pennsylvania. I remember there was an arcade nearby and she would give us money that Richard and I would spend trying to get little stuffed animals out of a claw machine. Both grandpas were gone but I am glad that both grandmas were able to meet us before they passed away.

11

Year One

Bill

ANNOUNCING A NEW BIRTH is one thing, but how does one proclaim to friends and family the sudden arrival of children aged 8 and 9? We crafted a simple announcement with a photo of Lillian and Richard and this haiku:

> Silence of waiting
> Suddenly ends with a sound:
> Laughter of children

We had painted and prepared the two bedrooms for the kids with bedspreads and stuffed animals and we moved our own bed into the den at the center of the house. We had no age-appropriate toys, books, or other childhood accoutrements, but soon after they moved in our friends threw a gift shower for them which must have seemed like Christmas and Fantasyland combined.

As you might imagine it was quite an experience to have two children suddenly parachuted into our home. The house seemed smaller and much noisier. There were none of the established family routines that are normally worked out over a period of years: house rules, wake-up and bedtimes, school lunches, homework, television, chores, and bathroom euphemisms. Our two cats seemed just as bewildered as we were. Adding to the fray was the fact that in their youngest years there had been very little stable parenting. I added up with Richard the number of men he had called "dad." I was number nine. Lillian had actually been pressed into a parental role herself. When we began family therapy, which was quite soon, their chief complaint was, "Who are these people trying to set limits on us?" They were accustomed to being co-adults.

Something that is missing when adopting older children is the attachment that normally emerges between parent and child through infancy and the early years. There just isn't the solid foundation of bonding to cushion the hurts and to serve as a seatbelt on the rollercoaster ride. We had nothing with which to compare the experience at the time. I understand this more fully now having since raised a baby—the deep fierce bond that emerges when you hold and rock and feed your children and watch them grow through the exciting milestones of the toddler years. A mutual love can and does grow with experience when older children move in, but it is more gradual and feels a bit like taking in small roommates.

Affection does flower, though. Something happens deep inside when your child snuggles up in your lap or comes running to you for comfort when frightened by thunder. When I was traveling away from home in the first year I remember noticing the new experience of missing our children. I have a fond memory of lying on our backs on the grass in our front yard looking up at the stars and describing the constellations that I had learned as a boy scout. There were many hours of sitting together over homework and reading stories at bedtime. What a remarkable experience to have someone so depending on you for safety, stability, and most of all love! There was also the joy of helping them experience so many new things: a first trip by train and plane, a sit-down "slow food" restaurant, seeing an ocean for the first time.

At the same time that first year was without question the most difficult thing we had ever undertaken. There was shouting and defiance, something neither Kathy nor I had experienced much at home in growing up. I used everything I had ever learned as a psychologist and human being and it helped, but still I felt woefully inadequate to the task. I had just been promoted to full professor and become the director of clinical training in the psychology department, further increasing the demands on me at work. When I got home and grasped the doorknob at night I felt like I was beginning my second shift and more difficult job. We had a warm and talented family therapist who was a faithful companion on the journey but the stress strained us both as well as our marriage. From morning through evening most waking moments were filled with the challenge and emotional rollercoaster of parenting these children who already had well-established personalities of their own and a history of more trauma than anyone should have to endure. By the end of the day we usually fell into bed exhausted.

We had been told by the state at the outset that standard procedure was to wait at least one year before proceeding with adoption. We were beginning to understand why. I no longer remember the details of what events led up to it but after Easter, just past the one year mark we hit bottom and decided that we just could not do this any longer. We felt worn down, unable to go on together. I felt a disturbing change in myself. My optimism, my "living as if" had faded. I had used up all my ideas, hopes, and energy. I wrote in my journal, "I have gone from not wanting to be a father to feeling very much a father. Yet we do not have a family. We have come to the end of the road with the children. I am clear that I do not want to jeopardize our marriage any further in hopes of making a family."

On a Thursday that April we kept an appointment with our family therapist and poured out our hearts. She listened supportively, understood that in a year of twice-weekly therapy we had tried everything we could think of, and she urged us not to say anything about it to the children until we knew what arrangements could be made. We scheduled a meeting for the next day with the social worker who had handled their case and set the process in motion to find a foster placement.

We stayed awake long on Thursday night and I wept through some of the most bitter pain I have ever experienced. I fully faced for the first time the reality of saying good-bye to these children. It was like grieving a sudden death, with a deep sense of loss and failure. Every door seemed closed and all was dark.

On Friday morning it was heart-rending seeing them off to school. Every normal little word or act brought a sting of pain. Richard on leaving said, "I don't want to leave you, dad! I want to stay here with you." Did he know at some level? We weren't sure what to expect from meeting with the social worker. Would they be taken away from us immediately? No, the State hoped to find a new home for them in two weeks to two months, and meanwhile they were to live with us, not knowing.

On Sunday morning we went to church to discover that there was a visiting minister, the pastor of our sister church in Mexico. Rev. Jorge Mata preached in Spanish with a member beside him translating, and his text was the end of the gospel of John where the risen Jesus appears for the third time. Pastor Jorge said that the first two appearances had been in Jerusalem, the holy city. This time his disciples had set out in a boat returning to their old familiar life of fishing, but to no avail. They had fished all night with no catch. Jesus appears on the shoreline, at first a stranger, and tells them to try again by throwing their nets on the other side. They do, and the catch is so large that it strains the nets. What this tells us, the pastor said, is that God is with us not only in the holy places but in the difficult work of everyday life, the times of failure, the plain and ordinary places. When we left the sanctuary we looked at each other and asked, "Did you feel like that was for us?" Both of us did. There was no promise that things would be any easier but it seemed clear that God had brought these children to us in the first place and would walk with us on the rest of the journey.

And so on Monday morning we called our therapist again with the embarrassing turnabout. "I'm so glad," she told us. "I haven't slept well all weekend. It just didn't feel right. But I don't know how the state will react. They may already have moved ahead." So we called the social worker who also sounded relieved. We met and she assured us that if we did go ahead with the adoption the state would be there for us to help if things got rough down the road.

The adoption was scheduled for the last court day in December. Judge Martinez told us that he saved adoptions for the final day before Christmas because it was one of the few joyful parts of his job. The man in a black robe got to be Santa Claus for once, and we went home as a forever family.

12

School Days

Lillian

A REALLY SPECIAL DAY was the one before Christmas when we finally were legally adopted in an actual courtroom with a judge. I was excited, truly feeling special and wanted as I had never felt before. We had a lawyer who was there just to represent my brother and me. At court I was given the option to change my name if I wanted to and I decided to change my middle name as well as my family name. As a kid I hated my middle name (even though later in school I would try out playing the viola). So I decided to change my second name to my adopted mom's first name because she gave me a second chance in life and I couldn't wait to have that mother and daughter relationship.

School had felt strange to me when we were still with our birth mom. It's hard to explain, but I felt like I was different from the other kids, that I was poor and walking a tight rope all the time. When we moved into my adopted parents' house I was in third grade and this time when going to school I felt on top of the world. I was not poor and not a victim anymore but free. You might think "That's great," which it was, but since I was not used to this new feeling I wasn't sure how to handle it. Suddenly I was one of the popular kids; I had a great group of friends to hang out with and no one else was allowed in. Our little group would go as far away as we could on the playground and we'd play basketball and "kiss," a competition for who could keep up the longest kiss with her boyfriend. I also turned into a bully! There was this one particular girl I always picked on. I did mean things to her and it hurts now to think about it. She probably never forgot or forgave what I did to her, for which I'm truly sorry. I hope that she is now having a good life.

In summers we went to a parks and recreation program at Mark Twain Elementary School that paired able bodied kids like us with children who had physical handicaps. I really loved that experience of helping other people. It left a huge impression on me and we went back for a couple more summers.

When I went to Jefferson Middle School I felt truly lost. In elementary school I had been a bully and high up on the popularity chain, but when I got to middle school I was quickly put in my place. I guess you could say I was trying to find myself and figure out who I was. I did have some good friends and was in talent shows and in chorus which I loved, partly because the chorus teacher was awesome. I was also in home economics. However, this was not a good time for me and it began a long and heartbreaking period for my parents who gave me everything. I broke all the rules and started to smoke cigarettes, sneak out, and just rebel in not wanting to be with them anymore because they had rules and would not let me do whatever I wanted. I do remember pestering my parents to let me get a second piecing in each ear, saying that all my friends already had them and I was out of it because I didn't. Finally they said OK and about a week later, without thinking, I blurted out, "Now that I have two earrings in my ears all my friends want to get them!" Oops!

It was actually in the summer before seventh grade when I was 13 that everything changed for me. I was at the Mark Twain program again, but this year was different. I was on a mission of finding a boyfriend because I didn't want to be alone. I was boy crazy like a person on drugs and would do anything to see a boy I liked. I would flirt with the lifeguards at the pool and was pretty sure they would flirt back with me but nothing ever came of it. There was one boy, though, who was a counselor which meant he was older than me. He liked me too and we would go and kiss where no one else could see. He was so nice to me and I thought that I loved him. I would sneak out of the house at night which was not easy. There were wrought iron bars on all the windows, but my parents had installed fire escape handles in each of the rooms to release the bars from the inside. I would open that to go out of my window and he would meet me down the road. He had someone else drive and it was scary. When we drove by a police car they would make me hide on the floor. We would go to his sister's house and when we got there we went straight to a bedroom and never hung out. That first night was when I lost my virginity in an unknown place while he was smoking a joint. I don't know why I would ever put myself in such an unsafe situation but I kept on doing it until I was caught.

Once I got caught I flew off the handle and told my parents I didn't want to live with them anymore, a decision I don't understand now because it seems like any kid would rather have parents than no parents. I broke all the rules, smoked cigarettes whenever I had the chance, snuck out, and just rebelled. I broke their hearts and was so mean to them. I don't know why I was so angry, but I was out of control. So they found a place I could go to, a local psych hospital that they hoped would help me. I was there for more than a month and still stuck to my decision that I did not want to live with them.

So when I was 13 I went to live at a place called Girls Ranch. There were two dormitories, one with the younger girls and the other for older girls. Our house had about eight rooms with one or two girls in each room and a live-in mom and pop. There were no doors, but we each had our own space. There were farm animals, a building where we got donated clothes and essentials, and a cafeteria where we would all eat together every day. During the week they took us to school and on Sundays we went to church. I lived in the younger girls' building and was never really close to the house parents though I knew they cared for each and every one of us. Sometimes I went to them if I had issues, but mainly I would talk to the other girls who had different stories of their own. Whenever we got into trouble we had to go and shovel horse manure, which was hard work. We had to do it even if it was raining and we were grounded until we got it done. How many wheel barrows we had to haul depended on what we had done. Once I shoveled with other girls and once I was out there by myself. It only took a couple of times for me to figure out that I had better follow the rules. The best impression and impact on me, though, was not from the house parents but from the other girls. I begged to be in the older girls' house and after a while it happened. A lot of those girls didn't like me because I was so lost, but they guided me and helped me figure out who I was and wanted to be.

While I was at Girls Ranch my parents helped me get into a private school because I hated the public school I was in. The private school was in a church with only one classroom as I remember. There was just one teacher and maybe five other kids in the class, and I loved it. I got along with the other kids and we would have youth groups and I was fitting in. There wasn't pressure to do the work, but we had a little cubby with lots of pillows where we would read and do all our school lessons, and at break we girls would give each other massages.

Although the staff took us to church every week I never really paid much attention to what was happening. Then one Sunday morning something just clicked inside me. I felt like a human being, someone who mattered and I started getting my life together and let God into my life. It was like a weight was suddenly lifted off my shoulders and I began getting along better with my housemates and house parents.

13

Down Under

Bill

IT WAS COMING TIME for me to take a sabbatical leave after 13 years on the University of New Mexico faculty when a colleague invited us to spend the year in Sydney, Australia where he directed the National Drug and Alcohol Research Centre. It would prove to be a fruitful year for me professionally, and this time it also afforded our family the adventure of a year living down under. We began making plans for Lillian and Richard to continue school in Australia, where the seasons are opposite to those in the Northern Hemisphere.

Soon after Lillian turned 13, however, some ghosts emerged from the closet in the form of painful memories and issues from her early life. We had all been in ongoing family therapy, but her rollercoaster emotions and utter rejection of parental limits led to five weeks in a psychiatric hospital, and it was unclear whether or when she would be returning to our family. By year's end she had begun a longer-term placement at New Mexico Girls Ranch, a multi-denominational Christian residential program near Santa Fe. Our visits were tense. "I am not like you," she insisted angrily. "You are not my real parents. I'm like my mother." In frightening ways it seemed to be true.

So we began planning to take only Richard with us to Australia that summer. We weren't willing to risk taking such a rebellious and unpredictable adolescent into a whole new culture for a year, nor was she interested in going. Again I felt such despair and failure. We arranged as best we could for our friends to visit and look after her while we were away.

A few weeks before we were to leave I drove up to Girls Ranch once again to visit Lillian, now 14. Kathy had felt so burned by previous visits that she didn't go along this time. Lillian refused even to see or talk to me, which really stung. I turned around and drove back home feeling quite hopeless. A few days later Lillian telephoned and said, "I need to see you, dad. Something has happened." She sounded different, so I made the drive again. When I arrived the change in her was plain. I experienced in her a very different person from the raging teenager of just a few days before. Something astonishing had happened. Sullen anger had been replaced with a peacefulness, a gentle acceptance of her situation. Most strikingly I experienced in her the abrupt appearance of a quality that I had not witnessed in her before: *empathy*, the ability to see the world and herself through the eyes and experience of others. For the first time she could appreciate and verbalize what we must be experiencing in our relationship with her. She seemed to have a settled peacefulness and a compassionate kind of maturity, and it had all occurred, she told me, within the space of a few minutes. She had been sitting resentfully in the back row of a mandatory church service, arms crossed, waiting for it to be over when something happened. She found it difficult to describe in words. It was nothing that she had expected, invited, or even wanted, and yet something had changed her. It was not anything she had done herself; it was more like something done to her, and it felt completely positive. I was skeptical, of course, and yet at a deep level I *knew* that this was a different girl. As I learned later and wrote about in the book *Quantum Change*, profound experiences of this Ebenezer Scrooge variety do happen in real life and are much more common than one might expect.

So now what? After discussing it with our friends, therapist, the ranch staff and Lillian herself, we decided to allow some time to see what the next few months would bring. If this change proved stable we would be willing to have her join us for Christmas and the rest of the year down under. By November everyone agreed that whatever change had occurred that day was continuing. Indeed, those qualities of confident calmness, compassion and empathic understanding remain with her three decades later. So in December she had the adventure of traveling unaccompanied across the international dateline on a twenty-hour flight to the land of Oz.

As will become apparent later, her enduring emotional and temperamental changes did not mean an end to problems or conflicts. Lillian is her own person, a clone of neither us nor her birth parents, and hard times still lay ahead. She is a survivor, though, moving through it all with the deep core of presence that came to her at the young age of fourteen.

The year was a rich experience for us all in the land down under where so many things are opposite. We arrived to winter in July, then Lillian arrived for a hot and muggy Christmas in the middle of summer. People drive on the left and pass on the right, and water spins down the drain counterclockwise. It's warmer in the north and colder in the south, everyone had free health care, voting was compulsory, and the conservative party was called the Liberals. On nighttime TV we watched the U.S. "Today" show live from yesterday.

At school Lillian and Richard enjoyed being the only "American kid" in their separate schools. Their elective options at public school included snorkeling, aerobics, golf and tennis. They quickly mastered the complex city bus system and we enjoyed exploring some of Sydney's ninety-three beaches. On road trips the two of them bickered in the back seat as we passed kangaroos and wallabies in the wild. In the far north we camped 150 miles from any city underneath a sky awash with the Milky Way. To me, having grown up in boy scouts, it felt deeply disturbing to look at the night sky and recognize nothing. The Big Dipper constellation appears only briefly in summer on the far northern horizon and upside down, being called the Plow.

When we returned to Albuquerque in June they were older (15 and 14), taller, tanner, and stronger. Hoping to reduce risky peer pressures on vulnerable mid-teens we enrolled them in a private Christian high school. We would soon discover that we were not the only parents with that idea.

14

Moving Out

Lillian

JUST BEFORE CHRISTMAS WHEN I was fourteen I rejoined my parents and my brother to live in Australia where my dad was working on sabbatical leave for a whole year. I flew there by myself and I don't remember being scared because my parents made sure I had help every step of the way. I remember getting off the plane and I expected to see kangaroos hopping all over the city. I was bummed that they weren't, but it was so pretty and such a different place from what I was used to in New Mexico. The people had strong accents and seemed pretty happy.

We lived in a three-bedroom townhouse in Coogee, a seaside suburb outside of Sydney. I remember not having much in my room except for a bed, a U2 poster and my radio but I never complained because it was awesome. I went to an all-girls school and was fitted for a uniform when I got there. The green skirt didn't fit very well and the black shoes were large and shiny. The school was full of kids from around the world so I was not the only girl who was different, although I think I was the only American which did get me a lot of attention.

I don't remember much about what we did academically. It all just seemed confusing to me, but I do remember being in a dance class and also a botany class that was very hands-on. We would walk around neighborhoods studying plants and trees. I pretty much stayed out of trouble, although sometimes I would ditch school with a couple of friends and go to the cemetery where we knew we would not get caught. My brother went to a different school that was co-ed and he didn't have to wear a uniform. That was OK; he had his friends and I had mine. I quickly got involved in a youth group through a church my parents found and I made really good friends who helped me stay in tune with myself and be happy. We did everything together and would hang out on the Coogee beach which was just a few blocks from where we lived. Richard's group joined us sometimes, too. We learned to body surf and I enjoyed stopping at a local shop on the way to the beach for fish and chips.

We did lots of traveling and exploring which is something my parents are good at: finding interesting things to do and having a plan. We went to zoos, fed kangaroos and held koalas. On the west coast we had the experience of dolphins swimming around us in the ocean, and on the east we snorkeled along the Great Barrier Reef. In downtown Sydney we saw lots of street performers, a couple of whom became friends and would come over for dinner at our apartment. In New Zealand we rented a camper van and drove around both islands. As a school assignment I kept a journal of my experiences, which included climbing on glaciers, visiting a kiwi farm and a Maori village. It was the most amazing experience, and I soaked it all in and enjoyed everything. I followed my parents' rules in Australia and we had a good relationship.

When we returned to New Mexico I was in the ninth grade and I went to Hope Christian High School where I got very involved and made a lot of friends. They were fascinated by my Australian accent, which disappeared quickly. I was on the junior varsity volleyball team that went to state finals that year. There were a couple of boyfriends but nothing serious and I wasn't allowed to date yet anyway. When I got my driver's license everything seemed perfect.

It was at Hope High that I met and fell in love with a tenth grader named Jeff and that's when things began to change for me once more. His parents were going through a divorce and he felt like he needed someone to love just like I did, so my old self came back. I wanted to be with him all the time, and when my parents didn't let me I started sneaking out the window again at night, only this time I had a driver's license and there was a car that I could take. My brother and I would roll the Festiva out of the driveway to the street so my parents wouldn't hear it start and we drove to Jeff's house which was pretty far from where we lived. There we would listen to music in his room or watch movies. I'm not sure if his parents even knew I was there because I arrived late and left while it was still dark so we could be back in our rooms before dawn.

Eventually I was caught again because my dad, who often doesn't pay much attention to details, noticed that the mileage on the odometer had changed overnight. Oops! As before I flew off the handle and told my parents that I wanted to be with Jeff and not live with them anymore. I ran away from home and went to live at his house. My parents would track me down and I would just run away again, so they sent me back to the psych hospital and that just made me madder at them and more determined to be with Jeff. While in the hospital I stayed in contact with Jeff and we would try to see each other. One time I convinced my parents to add a church friend to the visitor list and instead Jeff came, but the hospital staff quickly figured out that this was not the person who was supposed to be there.

So I worked my way up to the highest level of privileges so I could go on a community outing to the skating rink. I met Jeff there and we ran away, driving all over New Mexico in his new truck, trying to not be found. Jeff had his father's credit card that we used to get food and gas and stay in some motels until his dad discovered it and canceled the card. I was missing for a long time with my parents adamantly trying to find me, even hiring a detective. I knew that I was putting Jeff's family in danger of being in trouble with the law so eventually I called my parents and basically turned myself in.

That's when our former neighbor couple offered to take me in. They had two small boys for whom my brother and I had been babysitters. My parents said OK, and living with them was nice for a while. They tried to prepare me to be out on my own, and I followed their rules until I got pregnant. They wanted me to keep the baby and so did I. I started buying baby clothes. I went to my first prenatal appointment and had ultrasound pictures that I shared with my friends at youth group who were excited for me. Jeff, however, was thinking more about the reality of being teenage parents and how hard that would be. After talking it over we decided that it was best to terminate the pregnancy, which is the hardest decision I have ever had to face. I had wanted a baby of my own and here I was with one. When I lost the baby I also lost a piece of myself. The pain of going through the abortion was terrible and it's something that I never talked about. I know abortion is a very controversial subject on which people have strong opinions. I just ask not to be judged on the basis of one decision that we made when I was sixteen.

Anyhow when we made this decision the neighbors I was staying with said I could no longer live with them, so I moved in with Jeff's family for a while. My parents did not approve of this plan and they arranged for me to live in a group home to help me learn skills I would need to be on my own. I was the youngest person there and I had my own room in the basement which I remember painting bubble gum pink. I did like the program and felt like I was free to be an adult. There were groups mainly about drugs which I didn't relate to since I wasn't using any and never had. We also had to hold down a job and they taught us how to shop on a budget for food. Even though I was lost I did stick with my own goals which included not ever being like my birth mom. I was not going to be an alcoholic or use drugs and I would never abuse my kids.

I still was dating Jeff and we were very much in love. When Jeff turned 18 and was legally independent he decided to pack up what he had in his Chevy truck and move to Montana. I was only 17 but I was not about to have him going off without me, so two weeks later I ran away once again and headed north to join him.

15

Runaways

Bill

OUR AUSTRALIAN FRIENDS HAD found it incredible that in New Mexico children at age fourteen can get a learner's permit to drive and at fifteen have an independent driver's license. Even now the age for a learner's permit down under is sixteen, and seventeen for a driver's license.

When we returned from Australia Lillian was fifteen and so I began the task of helping both of them to learn to drive. The fall term at school went well, with tall Lillian playing junior varsity volleyball and singing in the school chorus. Anticipating the new drivers we bought a little Ford Festiva as a second car, and Lillian quickly demonstrated her ability to drive safely. When we flew to visit grandparents in Illinois at Christmas that year we did not realize it would be our last trip together as a whole family.

One morning in March as I started the car to go to work I looked at the odometer. As it happened I had noted the mileage the evening before and an additional thirty miles had appeared overnight. In the confrontation that followed we learned that our children had been leading double lives, with Lillian taking the car after we had gone to sleep and returning before we awoke. Trust broken, they spent three months in a psychiatric hospital while we sorted out what to do next and gradually learned the alarming extent of their nighttime activities.

Lillian, now sixteen, ran from the hospital and went missing for ten days. When a detective whom we hired finally found her hiding at the home of her boyfriend she still refused to return home or live by our rules. A sympathetic former neighbor told us that we just had not loved her enough, offering to take her in and accept permanent guardianship. That lasted for only five months without ever finalizing the paperwork for guardianship, so we were back in legal limbo. Lillian spent part of that year in a group home but on Labor Day she ran away again, this time to live with Jeff's grandparents in Montana. We struggled with whether to use the court system to force her to come back and, for better or worse, decided that to do so would accomplish little more than further estrangement. She did keep in touch with us by phone and letters, and the following year she turned eighteen becoming legally responsible for herself. That at least was a relief.

The details of Richard's situation are not part of this story. Suffice it to say that he also ran away and was missing for weeks. Remembering the social worker's promise of help if things became unmanageable we wrote a letter to the state's Children, Youth and Family Department from whom we had adopted them, expressing our sense of being unable to provide the necessary supervision and asking for their help in light of what they had known to be a difficult placement six years earlier. The social worker who handled the adoption was no longer with the department, and weeks passed with no response at all. When a response did come it was beyond our wildest imagining: we were served with a summons charging us with child abuse and neglect. The sole basis, we later discovered, was our letter pleading our inability to supervise him. In the New Mexico statute defining child abuse and neglect the very last of a long list of possible qualifying conditions was failure of a parent to provide a child with sufficient control and supervision. The state took temporary custody of him and we hired an attorney to defend us in court. The charge was subsequently dropped when we arranged to place him with a family and pay child support until he turned eighteen. He is now married, working, and raising a family back in Portales.

16

Up North

Lillian

RUNNING AWAY THIS TIME was different. Jeff drove up to Montana where his grandparents lived and a couple of weeks later his mom paid for me to fly up there with two suitcases of belongings. My parents didn't know about any of this, and I hated the idea of keeping them in the dark not knowing where I was and wondering if I was safe. I knew it hurt them so I ended up calling to let them know where I was, telling them not to worry. I guess at this point they gave up trying to get me back home, realizing that I didn't want to be there. They were tired of fighting.

In many ways Montana was wonderful. We loved being together in such beautiful mountains and forests. Living there was also hard, but I was with Jeff and that was all I wanted. We lived on his grandpa's ranch in a small camper trailer with no bathroom or kitchen, just a bed. We used the ranch's bathroom with a shower and mostly ate our meals at fast food restaurants. Jeff's uncle helped him get a job as a carpenter. I was working at a Wendy's restaurant, though usually we couldn't afford to eat there. Often we went to another place that sold really gross and greasy 25 cent hamburgers that made us wonder what kind of meat we were actually eating.

That winter in Montana was rough—bitter cold, so much snow, and long nights. Jeff had the only vehicle and he always had to be at work earlier than I did, so now I can truthfully tell my children that I had to walk a mile each way in a foot of snow to get to work. I doubt we would have stayed if we'd had to live in the camper all winter. Fortunately when it was coldest we were able to live in the house because his grandparents moved to Arizona for the winter. Jeff's aunt and uncle made sure that we kept things in good order and would sometimes come over to check on things.

Even though we had to work hard we also made time to enjoy life. The house was on a big hill and we would go sledding down the hill with some of the neighborhood kids. We made lots of friends through my work. My best friend there was so beautiful and she also had a long-term boyfriend. We did everything together and our boyfriends got along well, too. They introduced us to other people who became friends and soon we had our little group. We had plenty of parties, smoked a lot of pot, and sometimes took mini-thins, a pill for people with asthma that we could buy at the gas station. Taking about ten of them would give you a speedy feeling, basically like cocaine but cheaper, and I always told myself I would never take cocaine.

Several times we also got away to his grandpa's cabin, inviting our friends to go along. It was out in the Bear Tooth Range of the Rocky Mountains and was such a beautiful little place. We would go there to fish in the nearby stream and take long four-wheeler rides. In the process we got to see a lot of wildlife up close: moose, deer, as well as some close encounters with bears.

This move to Montana was my first experience of how life was going to be from then on. What I had been fighting for was the freedom to live as an adult. We lived poor and it was a rough year, but I don't regret moving to Montana because it was such a new experience trying to make it on our own.

After a year when I was about to turn eighteen we decided to move back to New Mexico where Jeff was going to help his mother with her landscaping business. He wanted to explore relationships with other girls, a couple of whom had been interested in him before we left. The drive back was agonizing for me knowing that we were not going to be together. I was crying and trying to talk him into staying together. I believed we could be just friends but I wanted more and I was not going to let him go that easily. Looking back now, I am not sure why I put myself through all that heartache, but I am glad that I did.

Before I turned eighteen I hadn't really thought much about meeting my birth mom. I was focusing on how I could make my own life better than hers had been. But then I started wondering what she looked like and whether she had got her life together, without any real expectations of having a relationship with her. It turned out to be easy to find her. Stockton is a relatively small town and I found a phone number for her mother, who knew where Terry was staying and gave me the number to call. I was nervous about talking to her but when I did call Terry almost acted like I had never left. She seemed to be in a good place in her life, with a boyfriend who was not drinking or drugging. I had not thought much about how our conversation would be but I did have three questions I had been wondering about. Is she still alive? Obviously she was. Is she off drugs? She said that she was. Do I have any other brothers and sisters? No. I also hoped to hear some sort of apology. I wasn't really angry at her for doing the things she did but I wanted to hear her acknowledge that she did wrong. However our first conversation was all about catching up on missed times.

After telling my parents about my conversation they offered to fly Richard and me out to visit Terry so we could get to know her better. They supported our knowing more about our birth parents. When Richard and I got to Terry's house she looked much as I remembered. Her voice sounded the same and so did her laugh. She and her boyfriend lived in a small comfy house so Richard and I slept in a camper they had in the backyard. We all talked a lot catching up on our life stories. My brother has always been good at making a stressful situation less awkward by getting everyone to laugh with his jokes. I on the other hand am a little more on the serious side. It was the first of several times I would see Terry, and I am glad we were able to go. After that I called her about once a month to keep in touch and see how she was doing.

17

Homecoming

Bill

IN 1993 A FEW months after her eighteenth birthday Lillian and Jeff returned home from Montana. She lived with us for a few months while working, pursuing her education, and preparing to live on her own. Then with excitement she moved into her first apartment, sharing the rent with a young woman from England while taking some community college courses with a dream of becoming a social worker. (I do remember Lillian playing social worker when she was ten or eleven, busily making calls on her toy phone to help place children in need of homes.) Once again we were able to enjoy Christmas together with both of our children, though this time without my mother who had died just before Easter.

So a new life experience began for us, relating to our children as adults. Once both of them were legally adults and responsible for themselves we could all relax a bit. Lillian began to develop close and affectionate relationships with both of us, even asking for advice on occasion. It's difficult to say just how this is different from parents' relationship with a child they have raised from birth, but it seems so. We received these children with already formed personalities just as they were about to tumble into adolescence, and so much of our early life together had been about struggling over limits that they rejected. That's part of the job description of an adolescent: to individuate, develop a personal identity that is separate from and yet still attached to parents. Without the normal buffer of attachment that develops in infancy the conflict was intense. Now mostly freed from that struggle, we began to explore what a relationship would be like with these unique individuals. It is said that you don't get to select your family but we actually did, or at least we said Yes when they were brought to us.

In 1995 I began awakening in the middle of the night and unable to get back to sleep, which is quite unusual for me. I would break into tears for no apparent reason and was having trouble concentrating at work. I was scheduled to co-chair a conference in the Netherlands and my energy was so low that I wasn't sure if I could do it. My normal pathological optimism was gone. It occurred to me that I had written about this phenomenon in textbooks but had never experienced it myself. I looked up the diagnostic criteria for depression and the picture was clear. But why? At least for a psychologist it's not hard to find plausible explanations. The behavior therapist I consulted was both compassionate and pragmatic and while we explored potential reasons she also had me start an antidepressant medication. We continued for several months and as the depression lifted my usual optimism and energy returned. I recognized the symptoms early when it recurred twice more in subsequent years, resuming therapy and medication with good results. As I reflect on it now, both my father and his father looked clinically depressed throughout their last decades, and I probably inherited a predisposition. At my doctor's recommendation I have stayed on a low dose of medication with no recurrence.

These episodes left me with an insider's empathy and compassion for depression and for suffering more generally, and I think the experience softened me in some ways. I look at the world with wistful appreciation and gratitude. Even at the very bottom I felt a kind of anchor holding me fast. I certainly felt tossed about and out of control but never feared that I would be lost. It is a gift of trusting faith that my mother gave me.

In 1996 came the day that any father dreams of with Lillian announcing that soon after her twenty-first birthday she would be marrying Jeff, her only boyfriend of five years. We made friends with the soon to be in-laws and I set to work on our back yard where the wedding would occur, followed by a reception at the home where Jeff grew up. The vision of Lillian in her white wedding gown is emblazoned on my visual and emotional memories. But I should not say too much about that because the story is Lillian's to tell.

18

Wedding

Lillian

AFTER JEFF AND I got back from Montana it was very rocky for a while. We would have times when we were not together but yet we would still hang out with each other as best friends and then end up back together again. We had the same friends and loved doing the same things. We did a lot of camping and fishing together. We loved being with friends and partying. We got our own apartment and Jeff took over his mom's landscaping business while I worked with special needs adults in residential settings. We both loved pets; we had dogs, snakes, fish, cats and a rabbit.

After being together for five years we were finally stable enough in our relationship for me to know that I wanted to be with him forever. So I told him that I wanted to get married; that if after five years he still didn't realize that I was the one he wanted to be with for the rest of his life, then I was going to go my separate way. It was at that point he agreed that we would get married. There was no special proposal, and eventually he gave me a ring.

When I told my parents they were happy for us, but they also had a lot of heartache and some hard feelings about how his parents had helped me hide and run away when I was younger. I remember my mom saying that they would have no part in this wedding unless we all sat down and had a talk about her feelings.

So we did! She said what was on her mind without hesitation, like a hibernating beast that had been waiting to come out for many years. For my mom's peace of mind Jeff's parents sat and just listened to some pain-filled words. From their point of view they had just been helping a homeless child; in my parents' eyes they were harboring and keeping a child from her home.

This meeting was a watershed and we could all move on from the past. Our parents, though different, could be friends. My mom and I developed the most amazing relationship after that meeting and she accepted me as an adult. Together we planned without disagreement the wedding that I had dreamed of. We did the things that every bride and mother go through: finding a beautiful dress, figuring out the cake and flowers, choosing the venues. Our wedding rehearsal dinner happened at a local club with great food and some lovely presents.

Then came the day: May 11, 1996, nine days after I turned twenty-one. The wedding was in my parent's backyard and it was serene. We walked down an archway of trees accompanied by my adopted dad and my step dad, Terry's second husband who had taken part in raising me. (I hope that makes sense—I know my life and family tree can be confusing.) We had a pastor whom I had known for a long time and my Uncle Don (my dad's best friend) sang "In my Life" by the Beatles. We wrote our own vows and Jeff cried when he said his. It was so perfect!

After that our wedding reception was at Jeff's mom's house where we did our toasts and our dance that Jeff and I had practiced with a friend who was a dance instructor. We took plenty of pictures and had lots of fun! Here is the toast that my dad offered that day:

> Those of you who are parents will understand what I mean when I say that life offers very few opportunities for parents to embarrass their children, so when one of these precious moments comes along, you never turn it down lightly. I have so many snapshot memories of this young woman stored in my heart. The very first is of watching the evening news with Kathy and seeing on Wednesday's Child two beautiful children in a pet store at Coronado mall. Lillian was embracing a basset hound puppy and the announcer was saying that like the puppy, these two

desperately needed a home. Somehow both of us knew at that moment that these were our children. I remember the first time we met. It was at the social services office in Clovis, and we were all nervous. How would it go? What do you say when you meet someone who may or may not become your child? The door opened and Lillian came straight to us, smiling. "Hi mom! Hi dad," she said and embraced us. I was blown away. I learned something about her that day, although it took years for me to understand it. Whenever life brings Lillian changes or fear, sadness or possibilities or the unknown, she reaches out and embraces it and says Yes. She is one brave and strong human being.

I remember a birthday party among the roses in our first back yard. She was riding piggyback on Richard's shoulders and she was having fun and letting go so completely and laughing so hard that Richard's shirt got wet.

I remember Lillian and Richard in a summer recreation program at Mark Twain School, where half of the children were physically disabled and half were not. Clearly in her eyes there were no real differences between them. She and Richard quickly joined those who cared for their disabled friends, doing the hard and dirty work of loving.

I remember a day when Lillian, as a young and independent teenager, was powerfully touched by God's spirit suddenly, unexpectedly, while she was in northern New Mexico. I saw the dramatic change in her and she had difficulty even finding the words to describe her experience. But she did not run from it.

I remember her first glimpse of an ocean. I remember her wide-eyed wonder as we visited on one long trip Australia, New Zealand, Fiji, and Hawaii, and she encountered the rich variety of human culture. "Well," she said as we flew home, "I guess now I've seen the whole world." And in a way she had.

I remember the day a few years ago when the phone rang and the voice at the other end said "This is Lillian and Richard's mother." And again through the pain Lillian reached out and embraced.

And now she reaches out to embrace this young man. You've got a live one on your hands, Jeff! She is full of curiosity and passion and compassion. May your life together be a continuing and joyful journey of embracing and being changed by all that you meet.

Our wedding was such a wonderful day and a start of our new beginning together. Jeff and I left the next day to Puerto Vallarta for a week-long honeymoon. We stayed at what seemed to me a very high-end hotel next to the ocean and spent a lot of time on the beach with fancy drinks in our hands. On a tour we rode horses that seemed way too small to a waterfall where we were the only ones there, swimming together and having a romantic time. We had a dinner with a local family in their hut. I helped the lady make tortillas and we drank Coronas. It was so awesome to be able to see what life and traditions are like there.

Jeff went paragliding but I stayed safe on solid ground. I am pretty afraid of heights so there was no way I was going to hang from a kite. He said he enjoyed it and also at times felt like he was in danger. We did some shopping and on the last day there I got my hair braided, which I loved. I had long hair then and there were two women working on me at the beach.

When we returned we went on with life as we knew it then. We had a nice apartment and we both had jobs. I was working at a pet store and Jeff was taking over the family landscaping business from which his mom wanted to retire. All that was before children.

19

Jayson

Bill

JUST TWO YEARS AFTER Lillian's wedding we were traveling when we received a telephone call from our son telling us that his seventeen-year-old girlfriend was pregnant and they were excited about having the baby. Jayson was born a few months later, our first experience with a new infant in the family. I have a vivid memory of sitting alone with him in a rocking chair one night in our dark and silent living room, the same chair in which my own grandfather had rocked me as a baby fifty years before. I remember a feeling of warmth and joy spreading through my chest and marveling at the perfection of tiny fingers and toes as he slept in my arms.

How eerily history can sometimes repeat itself across generations! Within a year Jayson's parents had split up, recapitulating Richard's own experience as a baby. Neither parent was really prepared to be raising an infant and Jayson was moving around with his birth mom. She called us one day when he was fifteen months old saying that she had pneumonia and could we take care of Jayson for a few days. Kathy drove over, picked him up, and brought him home. It was about six weeks before we heard from his mom again, and then it was just a phone call to say how she was doing without asking much about him. We learned later that the state had already filed a charge of child neglect.

During these weeks Jayson settled in. I remember that when I held him on the first day or two he would squirm around anxiously to look behind him, but before long he started nestling into my chest. Soon he began walking and talking. His first word emerged with a game that we played while he sat in his high chair. He would drop something on the floor and say, "Uh oh!" I would pick it up, put it back on his tray and he would drop it again, laugh, and say "Uh oh!"

The attachment that happens between parent and baby is fierce as well as joyful. My need to protect and nourish him felt as ardent as his need to be protected and nourished. I understand the image of a mother lifting a car to free her child. The strength of our bond took me by surprise. I knew in the abstract that parent-infant attachment is profound but I had never experienced it from the adult side.

After he had been with us for two months the phone rang again. It was his birth mother saying that she was moving to Texas with her new boyfriend and we should bring Jayson back to her. We hung up the phone and decided that the cycle had to stop with us. We hired an attorney and filed unopposed for temporary guardianship, then permanent guardianship. Soon after his third birthday we filed for adoption which was granted a few months later. He had been nana and pappy, but soon he began calling us mom and dad. Of course he still knew of his birth parents. His birth mother had visited only twice when he was a toddler, but over the years he retained a relationship with Richard as his birth father. "You are a lucky boy," I told him. "Most boys have only one father, but you have two."

For me raising Jayson from infancy through elementary school is one of the great blessings of my life. We got to experience the very span of childhood that we had missed with our older children, and it somehow completed a circle. He loved for me to lie down with him at bedtime and tell him a story or sing to him. One night he asked me to sing the "body lotion" song, which puzzled me. It turned out that he wanted "My Bonnie lies over the ocean"! There were all the firsts that are so magical. His first sentence—"Ball go"—accompanied by a forceful pitch that foreshadowed his love of sports. Again we were present to witness this little human's first experience with an ocean. We had a fun ritual of him snuggling in between us in a "Jayson sandwich" as we stood hugging. I ran behind as he learned to ride a bicycle, and much later had the delight of introducing him to cross-country skiing. Before long he was beating me up the hills, which was not all that difficult as I was 60 at the time. Emulating my father I became a scout leader and we went camping and adventuring together.

Jayson turned out to be an intrepid traveler. I vividly recall him at age three pulling his own little roll-aboard bag through the airport with a teddy bear perched atop. By eleven he had been in twelve countries with us thanks in large part to travel opportunities afforded by my work. On one of the first trips we spent two weeks in Santa Margherita, Italy. As we began packing up to leave the hotel Jayson looked crestfallen: "I thought we moved here!" he said. It is still a joy to travel with him.

All this was not without its difficulties, pain, and angst. As he grew older he put dents in the floor and punched holes in walls and doors. Raising children liberated in me depths of emotion that I never knew I possessed. Genetically Jayson and I are very different people. Both he and Richard are more like my father and I wish they could have known each other. Yet the profound inexpressible bonds of attachment do smooth over the rough places, covering them with layers of love like blanketing snow. One day I wrote this for Jayson:

KITE

I hold your tether to ground; you chafe against it,
gently at first in halting, pulsing tugs,
and then in steady earnest as you find
the wind, and air fills out your sturdy frame.
Climbing, diving, dodging, turning, twisting,
you struggle mightily to wrestle free.
Indeed the wind would carry you away
and dash you from the sky like Icarus,
except my grip is firm, my footing strong,
and thus entwined we fly. Soar, boy!

When Jayson was eleven Richard told us "I'm ready now to take care of my boy." Words from the book of Hosea haunted me: "How can I give you up? How can I turn you over?" And yet it seemed to all of us the right thing to do, and in some ways symbolized a reversal of Richard's own childhood abandonment. They are so alike, these two boys of ours, and there are bonds of blood as well as of shared experience and loving. We remained his legal parents and once again I assumed the honored title of Pappy.

20

Wyatt and Sydney

Lillian

WHAT I ALWAYS LONGED for was a family to call my own, a family where I had some control and people loved me unconditionally. My adoptive parents did love me so much, but I couldn't really understand why they did because I thought I was broken, not savable. I realize now that other people can't really give you that feeling of control or being lovable if you don't accept and earn it yourself. It's like being a parent. Making a baby is simple enough, but being a mother or father is something that you earn by doing, by loving. I knew I'd had a hard life and I wanted to raise my kids in a healthier way of living, to make my life right in my own eyes. So we moved to the country and our first house was a double-wide mobile home on two acres across the Sandia Mountains from Albuquerque. We loved it out there with the open space, privacy, and actual winters with snow. Soon we had dogs, turkeys, and goats with kids of their own.

From the day we got married we started trying to get pregnant. We wanted to start a family right away but it was taking longer than we expected. Then one day I bought a home test kit and it read positive, so I went to our doctor to take another test and it also came back positive. I was excited to go for my first pregnancy visit, the one where they listen for the baby's heartbeat. They couldn't find one. An ultrasound showed that the sac was just empty—no fetus there. It was a false pregnancy. A few days later I had a DNC and I remember crying all the way home, so hard that I couldn't talk or even look at Jeff. I wanted a baby so badly.

About a year later we got pregnant again and this time I made it to full term, doing everything I was supposed do and keeping every doctor's appointment. Unfortunately I also gained a hundred pounds. I thought since I was so skinny and fit before that it wouldn't matter how much I ate while I was pregnant. Wrong!

We were blessed with our son Wyatt in 1998. Our parents were excited to have another grandson. My dad was the first person to get to the hospital, and he didn't want to put Wyatt down. We were so excited to show off our beautiful child to the rest of our family. There were lots of challenges with being a new mom, but he was perfect and everything we wanted. Jeff was already busy running his very successful landscaping business so we decided I'd be a stay-at-home mom. It was so fun to watch Wyatt grow each and every day. He had a hard time nursing and was a little jaundiced, so the first week we had a check-up every day. As new moms will understand, I hated to see them poking his tiny foot so many times.

Our Wyatt was all boy. He loved to climb and run and get into everything. We called him Dennis the Menace (after the cartoon character who was always getting into trouble), but then he would bat his big blue eyes at us and we couldn't even remember why we were mad at him. He was smart and hit each developmental milestone right on time. I read to him every day and night as he learned how to count, then learned the alphabet and began reading.

We planned for our children to be spaced a couple of years apart and Sydney was born in 2001 when Wyatt was two and a half. The pregnancy had gone smoothly. I was careful not to gain so much weight this time, still kept all my prenatal appointments, and took vitamins. She moved around a lot in there, like she was doing somersaults and having parties. The delivery, however, was not so simple this time around. Sydney's heart rate kept dropping and they gave me oxygen. There was all this beeping and people came running into the room. Jeff was just coming out of the bathroom when the doctor told me that Sydney needed to come out *now* and I should push or they would have to do an emergency

C-section. He tried forceps first, then a vacuum, then the forceps again this time putting his feet on the bed for leverage as he pulled. The umbilical cord had wrapped around her neck and arm so that every time I would push she was choking. Finally she came out and began to cry and everything returned to normal except for some bruising from the difficult delivery. We were excited to have the first girl in the family. We stayed in the hospital for two days and I remember another woman crying because she had just lost her baby. I was so thankful that Sydney had made it.

Having a baby and a toddler together was quite a struggle and I was glad I could stay home to teach and play with them. I was worried that Wyatt might be jealous but he quickly became a doting big brother bringing Sydney toys, playing with her, singing to her, and even helping to feed her after she was no longer nursing. Soon we enrolled Wyatt in a private Christian preschool so he could also get more socialization. He made friends quickly and I wound up volunteering with the school and running their fall festival for two years. Wyatt loved listening to music loudly with his dad. In fact it become a nightly ritual with the two of them jamming out and dancing while Wyatt played on his toy guitar or air guitar until bedtime.

When Sydney was about a month old and still tiny, Jeff's mother noticed that at times she would be looking at us but didn't seem to respond to our voices in any way. We consulted with her pediatrician and were referred for developmental testing. After a few months an evaluator came to our home, tested Sydney for age milestones, and noticed the same thing: she didn't seem to be responding to voices.

A first step was to test her hearing and I wondered how they would do this with a child who didn't seem to respond to sounds. They put us in a silent room with little stuffed animals arranged around it. If she looked at an animal when a bell sounded from that direction it would mean that she could hear it. She did.

Next we went to the neurologist who ordered an EEG and several scans. Then we went for genetic evaluation where they took measurements of every part of her body from head to toes, then drew a blood sample. While waiting for the results we continued to make memories and live our life. We went traveling, fishing and camping. Finally when Sydney was about a year old we learned that she had epilepsy. She had been having petit mal seizures and quite a lot of them. Jeff and I disagreed about whether to start her on antiepileptic medication. He was reluctant to give her such a harsh medicine and didn't think the seizures were really hurting her. I trusted the doctor's recommendation but we needed to be on the same page as her parents and so we waited a while longer.

It was when Sydney began to walk that we noticed she was falling a lot. She would be standing up and suddenly just fall down, often hitting her head. The doctor diagnosed drop seizures and ordered a helmet for her to wear so she would not hurt herself. The helmet took a while to arrive and by the time it did she had nearly outgrown it. The seizures were becoming more frequent so we decided to start her on medication to control them. We tried five different medications before settling on the two that she takes now.

Sydney continued to develop very slowly. We placed her in a public developmental pre-school that was a great program. She was able to get the treatment she needed right there at school and they helped us find resources and learn how to teach her basic life skills like brushing her teeth and using the bathroom. When she got to kindergarten she was tested again to make an individual educational plan. She was behind on all levels of cognitive, speech and physical development, but still the only diagnosis we had was epilepsy. When she was assessed again four years later I pressed for a diagnosis and was told that she was moderately mentally retarded. It's hard to explain how I felt when I heard those words. I had waited so long to have a name for why Sydney was the way she was, as if a diagnosis would make it better. Instead I cried all day. I guess mental retardation is what they say when they really don't know why your child has developed so slowly. Genetic testing didn't reveal anything unusual in us or her. With our permission they sent off a blood sample to some specialists in England who called two years later to say they had found something unusual but didn't know what it was. Maybe someday they will find out and offer something helpful to parents like us. The term "mental retardation" is no longer a proper diagnosis; now it is called intellectual developmental disorder. It still makes me so mad when someone is called "retarded," as if they were stupid instead of just being different.

One day when Wyatt was four I went to pick him up at preschool and there was a social services worker waiting for me. He had looked up a girl's skirt on the playground and in order to take him home I had to agree for him to be evaluated by a professional therapist. The worker also followed me home to check that the children were living in a safe place and told us that Wyatt could have no contact with any grandparents until they were also interviewed by social services. If we didn't follow through with all this the children would be taken away from us. I was devastated, hysterical. I kept asking God, "Why is this is happening to me all over again? Why do I have to keep going through this? It's not fair!" Of course this time I was a parent and not a child. My children were my world and there was no way I would let anyone hurt them. After several stressful months the state found that no harm or wrongdoing had occurred and the case was dropped. We withdrew Wyatt from the Christian school and were warned to be more careful about what we talked about in front of him. Do I still feel bitter about my family being put through such heartbreak? Sure I do. Mostly though I let go of it and moved on. I know that as a child I needed the protection of social services. So we got over this hurdle of life and Wyatt continued to grow. In fact he developed with a joyous spirit. He loved to fish with us and soon became quite a fisherman himself.

In 2005 we moved to a new home in the Sandia mountains. For some reason I thought we needed more space than we had, and we went from a mobile home to four bedrooms and three baths on three acres. It didn't take long to fill up the extra space and now I had a lot more property to clean and maintain in addition to taking care of the children and animals.

By the first grade Wyatt was already having a hard time in school. He was delayed in reading and math and began having behavioral problems. Frustrated by his learning disability he would get in trouble for saying bad words, fighting, and being defiant with his teachers. This type of behavior followed him into middle school and he already had a bad reputation in our small community. The school had little tolerance for misbehavior and was not well prepared to cope with more challenging kids. By this time his attitude toward school was that he just didn't care anymore. He was tired of teachers criticizing him, tired of feeling like he was different from other students. He seemed to feel a need to keep up his reputation as a bad kid by acting the way people expected him to. He also started smoking in middle school. We were smokers ourselves and did our best to keep cigarettes away from him but he always seemed to have a supply. When his friends came over we would check their backpacks (with parental permission) and before long no one wanted their kids to come over. We decided our best option would be to home-school him. It was expensive to buy the books and curriculum to use with him every day but he got through seventh grade this way.

Meanwhile Sydney's seizures were not getting any better. She had a friend in elementary school who had a vagal nerve stimulator (VNS) and we decided to check that out. The doctor did more tests and concluded that she was a good candidate for a VNS, saying it might decrease her seizures by half, possibly even enough to reduce her medication. Sydney was in 5th grade when she had the surgery and it was a long healing process but I'm glad we went ahead with the implant. When after a couple of years she complained about the wire hurting her we tried turning the VNS off for a while to see whether it was really working. Another EEG showed that it had been helping, so we turned it back on and she did not complain about it after that.

In eighth grade Wyatt asked to go back to school. He had a positive attitude and really wanted to try it again, but soon he was back getting into fights and trouble. A judge ordered him into anger management classes. His teachers didn't seem to want or know how to work with him, so again we withdrew him and I home-schooled him through the 8th grade.

The next year he wanted to go to high school and not do homeschooling anymore. I was certainly ready for him to move on and let him try it. He could have a fresh start in a new school that had some special needs services. Unfortunately his records followed him into high school resulting in a very restrictive individual educational plan. He was separated from most people his age, isolated with other high-problem kids, and soon was doing whatever he could to get out of school work. Reading was particularly hard for him, which in turn affects almost every other subject. I was frustrated that the school didn't seem to know how to work with him, in contrast to our wonderful and helpful experience in Sydney's schools. He never really got a chance to succeed there. Ever since elementary school not a week went by without a phone call from the school telling us what bad things our son had done. It just wears you down. Some days I would not even answer the phone.

In high school Wyatt also began taking pills, drinking, and smoking pot, having fallen in with peers for whom this was the norm. We got better at telling when he was on drugs: it made him have crazy eyes and he was rude and short, acting weird. We considered sending him off to a residential treatment center and came close many times, but figured it wouldn't do much good if he didn't want to be there. So once again we pulled him out of school for his safety, resumed homeschooling, and got him into some counseling. We hoped this would solve the problem but in spite of our efforts he kept in touch with the same friends who influenced him.

Through all of this I gained a lot of weight. I tried lots of diets and would lose but then go off the diet and gain it all back plus more. My highest weight was 340 pounds and it was really affecting my life with the kids. I couldn't do a lot of the things my family wished I could do, like going on long hikes and enjoying the outdoors. Jeff hated that I would sit on the couch and eat but he never really criticized me and he said I was still sexy to him. I began exploring weight loss surgery and found a Mexican clinic that was less expensive. Since our insurance wouldn't pay for it this seemed the only way we could afford it, so I talked to my parents about it and they said no way should I do that. They went with me to a seminar on gastric surgery options and they offered to pay for it. I had an all-day individual appointment to help decide which surgery was most suitable for me to lose the most weight and keep it off, and decided that gastric sleeve surgery was what I wanted because it had fewer side effects and problems. After this appointment I had to stop smoking and go on a two week liquid diet to show the doctors I was serious about changing. It was a very hard two weeks. Every time I wanted to smoke I would drink some decaf hot tea. I took the protein shakes they recommended and got through it.

Soon I was in a Texas hotel with my mom, waiting for surgery the next day. I was nervous, but I had been waiting for this for such a long time and I wanted a new way of life. When they released me after surgery my mom drove me home. I slowly went from a liquid diet to baby food and then regular food, and my family helped me develop a whole new way of eating. In the first year I lost 140 pounds and I felt like a new and happy person. It's been more than three years now and I've only regained ten pounds that I want to lose again because even that much of a gain I can feel. I will not throw this away.

Back to the kids. One day Wyatt flipped out on me for some reason, began yelling at me and I was yelling back. He got in my face and at one point I thought he might hit me but instead he punched a lamp on the wall. Glass flew everywhere and his hand began bleeding badly. I told him to get out of the house and I locked the door. He was outside literally foaming at the mouth, crying and mumbling. I had often thought about calling the police before and this time I did it for his safety and mine. By the time they arrived he had calmed down but clearly was still upset. They handcuffed him and he stayed calm. They talked to him and then asked if I wanted to press charges, which I did not. I just wanted him to learn a lesson and have his hand bandaged. They put him in the back of the cop car and scared him a bit. Then an ambulance arrived, taking him to have an evaluation and get his hand fixed. This turned out to be a wakeup call for him. He realized how he was treating his family and that it was the drugs and not him. After that he went faithfully to drug counseling and we told him if that was not enough he would have to go out of state for treatment.

Things got better after this incident. I wish I could say that it solved all of our problems but of course it didn't. It was just better. Wyatt became a more caring person and continued to learn from his struggles, for which I am grateful. We all have our challenges, and learning from them is what matters.

Sydney has grown a lot, too. She got into a middle school program with teachers who really worked with her on the behavioral problems she was having with other children and adults. The teachers and her therapist soon figured out that when she did things like pinch someone or pull their hair she would get immediate attention, even though it was negative. They also realized that when she had a seizure it would interrupt whatever she was thinking or doing and she'd get off track. They really helped Sydney feel like a normal child because they saw and treated her that way. Within a year her behavioral problems were essentially gone. That school was one of the best things for Sydney and provided real support for us as well.

We have been through a lot with our own kids and still it has been so fulfilling. Jeff and I have had consistent love and support from our families and from friends we made along the way. It really does take a village, and I could write a whole book just about raising Wyatt and Sydney. Having children, a family of my own, is what I most wanted. I never knew how hard it was going to be. I had fantasies about a perfect family in a home with a white picket fence and that's not how it goes. Sometimes I feel sorry for myself and ask why God gave me so much to handle. I feel overwhelmed about once a month, but I've learned a lot and become a stronger woman. I think God gave me these children because I can handle it; I'm the right person to give them the love and understanding that they need. My job is to raise my kids as best I can, keep them safe, help them feel wanted in this world, and prepare them for life as adults.

21

Away and Home Again

Bill

THE PHONE CALL CAME on Jayson's 16th birthday. He had run away from home in Carlsbad, New Mexico and went missing for eight days after his father discovered that he was dangerously involved in drug use. "I had never seen my father cry so hard," Jayson would later tell me.

It's difficult to describe the terrible feelings of dread that come when your child is missing. I hoped that the phone would ring, and especially at night I was afraid that it would. Eventually he turned up in a homeless shelter here in Albuquerque. A chaotic year ensued lost in the world of drugs, in and out of programs and shelters, with two crashed cars and a young girlfriend with a toddler in tow.

We called the police one crazy night when he began breaking out the windows of his dysfunctional car in our driveway. I was impressed with how well the officers handled the situation. They took him to an emergency room where he was placed on involuntary hold. From there he went to a locked adolescent psychiatric ward for stabilization and evaluation. Within days he looked unbelievably healthier. One of the best things they did there was to give him comparison photographs of himself upon admission and at discharge, pictures of two entirely different people.

He agreed to go voluntarily to a month-long residential treatment program in Texas. We walked out of the locked hospital ward together as a family, drove to the airport, and I flew with him to Dallas. He could have run at any time along the way but he didn't. He still looks back on this as one of his best treatment experiences. We drove down to visit him and talked with staff there. He looked at the before and after photos of himself and pointing to the former told us, "I *never* want to be back there again!" At the end of the month I flew back to pick him up and we attended a Narcotics Anonymous meeting together on the way to the airport.

Back in Albuquerque his sobriety lasted less than a day. Reconnecting with the same friends he was quickly using again and not following through with aftercare. Late one night we got a call from the juvenile detention center where he was being held. The next morning he was assigned a juvenile probation officer and released. More trouble soon followed: detention, trials, and another round of residential treatment. In truth this court-ordered program offered nothing resembling evidence-based treatment, yet "failure to respond to treatment" (in this case, refusing to take a medication) constituted a violation of his probation that returned him to detention and eventually a one-year commitment/sentence to a secure youth diagnostic and development center. We visited him there every Saturday for three hours when we were not traveling. I wrote to him about twice a week and received from him what few parents do these days: dozens of handwritten letters. Two Christmases and his seventeenth birthday passed. As his commitment time neared an end he was transferred to a less restrictive community reintegration center. As his eighteenth birthday approached I asked him what he was looking forward to most upon release. "Opening a door," he replied. It is the simplest of acts, but he had not done it for a year and a half. The symbolism was also not lost on me.

I have seen quite a few changes in Jayson, and he sees them himself. First there were the big changes that come with detoxification, just getting the drugs out of the system and allowing the body time to readjust and heal. One day at a time he accumulated more than a year of sobriety, even though drugs are still accessible when incarcerated. In that time he grew up a lot. Drugs have a way of stopping normal growth of personality and character, not only for adolescents but in adulthood as well. With sobriety even the brain can rebound physically, enlarging and growing denser with nerve cell connections. He became less impulsive and more able to stop and think before acting—the ability that we call self-control. As I noticed with Lillian long ago I have seen Jayson also grow in empathy, the ability to understand a situation from someone else's perspective.

So how do our children learn self-control? Consider this study from psychological research on parenting styles. A young child and parent were seated together in a room in which there was a table containing many wooden blocks of various sizes. The child was told to build a tower of blocks as tall as possible; the parent was given no instructions and they were then left alone together in the room. The focus of the study was on what parents do in that situation. Some just sat back and watched or ignored, letting the child play and offering no help. Some gave lots of directions or even stepped in to construct the tower themselves: "No not that way! That won't work. Here, let me do it." In between these permissive and controlling styles were parents who acted more like guides. They watched with interest and let their children try out different approaches but at key moments they would offer a bit of advice, which interestingly they often whispered in the child's ear. "Put the big blocks on the bottom." Then they would sit back again and let the child try. These were the parents whose children showed greater self-control on other tasks, more so than those whose parent was either hands-off or take-control. It's a tricky balance and we're bound to make mistakes, but underneath it all is a safety net, the firm assurance that "I will always love you no matter what comes."

Jayson was released shortly before his eighteenth birthday. When we arrived home I handed him the key as we walked up to the front door. He grinned remembering our conversation, unlocked the door, and stepped inside the home where he grew up. And then for five minutes he wept as Kathy and I silently enfolded this now large and muscular fellow in a Jayson sandwich.

22

Three Generations

Lillian

PEOPLE WHO ARE CARING for children of their own as well as older family members are sometimes called a "sandwich generation." When Wyatt was just a few months old I got a phone call that my own half-brother, now twenty, had been rushed to a hospital in Albuquerque diagnosed with an aggressive brain tumor that required quick surgery. He had no memory of Terry; the only mother he had known was his grandmother, so Jeff and I decided it was time for him and his birth mother to see each other. We paid for Terry to come to Albuquerque by bus which was less expensive than flying, and late one night we picked her up together because the bus station is in a rough part of town and it was already snowing hard. Driving back home through the mountain pass we could hardly see the road, so it took a long time but also made for an exciting trip.

This was the first time Terry had met either Jeff or Wyatt. This time she was in my world so I felt more comfortable than on our first visit. She also got to meet my mom and dad who invited us all over for dinner. She thanked them for doing such a good job in raising Richard and me and after a while I think she felt very comfortable with them, feeling no judgment. My parents have a way of doing that with people.

Terry stayed with us in our home and when our half-brother was out of surgery we went to visit him several times. He didn't show any emotion and I don't think he remembers much about these visits. He mostly needed to sleep, but it was nice to have the three of us kids together again, listening to music or just sitting with him quietly.

Meanwhile I was hoping to make some new memories with Terry, renew some trust and do some things we had missed out on as mother and daughter. Don't ask me why because for some people once that trust is gone you don't give it back. I guess I wanted to give her a second chance and the benefit of the doubt by trusting her again. One experience made it clear to me that she was not going to be the parent I hoped for. I asked her to help me with Wyatt by giving him a bath, to wash and play with him while I did the laundry and made dinner. A while later I saw her sitting by herself in the living room. "Where's Wyatt?" I asked, and she said he was playing in the bath! It may only have been for a few minutes but that's all it takes. I was boiling mad but I didn't confront her. I just made sure I never asked her to watch Wyatt again, and I realized we would never have the kind of relationship that I have with my adopted mom. The feeling came back from when I was young that I had to be on my toes and take care of everybody, never really knowing what to expect next. I could not say no to her, and I felt like it was my duty to take care of her since she was my birth mom. I also took on the job of caring for my half-brother for a year while he recovered from the brain surgery and had to re-learn the basic skills of walking, talking, and taking care of himself.

Terry would call periodically after that but I had completely lost contact with my birth dad Richard. With some help from a lady who was good at finding people I located him in California. His sister later told me that she had found Richard sleeping under a bridge using drugs, and she took him home to live with her even though she was in a one bedroom apartment with four kids. She had fed him and given him vitamins to help him get through withdrawal. In the process he met, married, and moved in with one of her friends. That's when I got his phone number and called him. He was very surprised and sounded happy to hear from me, so we talked and caught up on how we had been for all those years.

Through his whole life he had struggled with alcohol, meth and heroin and had been in and out of jails. He came to visit us in Albuquerque and stayed with my brother, his son Richard. They really hit it off drinking and hanging out together. The car he drove had broken down and we had to help him get it towed and repaired. Not long after that visit his new marriage broke up and he moved in with his sister who was also going through a divorce herself. She told me that soon after that she kicked him out when he stole her purse for drug money. Later on when he was hospitalized she went to see him hoping for an apology, but he said only, "Life is short and you should forgive me."

Another time Terry called to say she was on her way to see me. She had broken up with her boyfriend and was hitch-hiking to our house. Jeff and I were furious. I have a family of my own and don't want that kind of instability in my life anymore. I was mad at myself, too, because I still felt like I needed to help her and couldn't tell her no. This time she arrived with only $100 and no plans on leaving. She was with us for ten days eating our food and the $100 didn't begin to cover her case of beer a day. We did do some things together. She showed me how to make tortillas and she helped clean the house. I finally found the courage to tell her that we could not keep buying her beer every day and she had to work out her own plans, but we would buy her a bus ticket back to California.

After this I didn't hear from her for a year or more and during these long waits I would always wonder if she was alive or dead. When she did call sometimes I couldn't even understand her. I caught on that she was back to drinking and prostituting for drug money. She had hepatitis and her liver would swell up as if she was pregnant. Sometimes she would start treatment but didn't stick with it long enough to get well. This left me on an emotional rollercoaster. She finally got another boyfriend who took good care of her. They seemed happy, got married, and they were living in a mobile home in Alabama. His family and kids accepted her and she made some good friends in the neighborhood.

Then he passed away and her life fell apart again. She had to move out of the mobile home and was really depressed. Jeff and I offered to help her get into a house and apply for disability. I thought she would go for the idea, but the next phone call was from a hospital in Alabama. She had shot herself in the head, and they told me that since I was the oldest child it would be my decision whether to keep her on life support. I cried hard. I called my brother and we decided together to continue life support. She was not expected to live, but she did come out of the coma, remembered us and what happened, and began rehabilitation. A social worker got her into housing and onto disability income. We talked regularly and she was getting stronger, but then the calls came less often. The last time I heard from her she was staying with a girlfriend back in Stockton. I could tell she was back on heroin. The next call was from her sister telling me that Terry had died just one day before her 54th birthday.

My birth dad Richard is also gone, but before he died he stopped in to see us once more while on a road trip with a new lady, two cats, and all their worldly possessions. They stayed with us for a couple of days, got to see how my family lived, and I believe he got a feeling for who I am. We went through all my old photos and he told me some stories. A few years later at the age of 60 he died of hepatitis.

Now that both of my birth parents are gone and I've been working on this book I realize how all of this affected me much more than I knew at the time. I just got through it all doing what I needed to do one day at a time. My goal now is to be the best mom I can be for my own children so that the pain doesn't continue being passed from generation to generation, and in that I feel pretty successful.

23

Retiring

Bill

As I write this I am ten years into retirement from the University of New Mexico where I spent my entire faculty career. Several streams converged on 2006 as the right time for me to retire, and I announced my intention years in advance so that there would be ample time to turn over my responsibilities and ensure that no one lost their job in the process. No one did. In fact life there went on quite well without me. During the first few months I was licking my wounds about no longer being in the center of attention and responsibility until it hit me that that's the point of retiring! Now I have no employees, grant applications, budgets, deadlines, administration, clients, supervision, professional conferences, students, classes, or faculty meetings. I didn't realize how much weight I had been carrying until I put it down.

When I announced my intention some colleagues asked with astonishment, "But what will you *do*?" as though work were the only meaningful way to spend one's time. I concluded that people who ask that should not retire, or at least are not ready to do so. I wanted to follow the example of *Tonight Show* host Johnny Carson: to retire before they hope you do. For me, the answer to "What will you do?" is to experience life.

Some say that I have not really retired. After all here I am writing yet another book. For many the image of retirement seems to be of sitting in a rocking chair watching television, and I am not doing much of that so far. I still love to travel now that I don't have to. I still love writing now that I no longer need to publish. I miss my students and teaching and have found different ways to nurture others. I am engaged in our congregation's ministry with the homeless. Music has always been an important part of my life and now I have time to compose for choir. I loved what I did and I love what I'm doing. I suppose "semi-retired" is a good description.

There is a joy in letting go, in releasing what you love. The few really ugly retirements I have witnessed were those in which people fought to hold onto as much control as possible until the very last, sometimes vying to continue controlling events even after their retirement or death. There comes a point in life to begin turning over the reins and innovations to the next generation. Doing so is not the end of life; it is the beginning of the second half of life.

Letting go of our children is also vital. What a struggle this was for us through Lillian's adolescent years reflected in earlier chapters! In preparing for adulthood children naturally try their wings, pull against the kite string. It was not always clear whether we should be trying to rein her in or be giving her more freedom. Like adults, adolescents learn both by meeting firm limits and by trial and error.

I find that the view from the far side of parenting children is wistful. There are no perfect parents and surely there are things we could have done differently and better. What I cherish is the uncommon depth of bond between parent and child. We opened our hearts and our lives to forge such a relationship with three emerging people who needed a home. There is no other adult with whom we share the kind of connection that we have with our three children, having been through some pretty rough waters together.

Lillian now makes her own way in life. It is an odd and paradoxical experience, walking side by side with one's children on different journeys. Last year she and her family moved away from New Mexico to begin a new adventure. We still stay in close touch, of course, through copious communication media, and yet I feel a dull ache within me as if something important is missing or incomplete. Of all the losses that come with aging this is a kindhearted one, arising not from want but from an abundance of loving.

24

Moving On

Lillian

For a long time Jeff and I had dreamed of doing something different. We were just scared of moving into the unknown. The Albuquerque landscaping business that Jeff had been building since he was 16 was going well and we had a secure life with a big home, nice vehicles and pretty much everything we wanted. We were living in a pleasant small community in the mountains with both of our families near us, though we didn't visit all that often. We were all so busy; Jeff's dad was a successful salesman and his mom a traveling flight attendant. My parents volunteer in the community, travel a lot, and also raised my nephew Jayson, which as a grandparent can take a lot out of you.

Even though we were comfortable in our lives we also felt stagnant, like we needed a change. Jeff's body was wearing down from hard physical labor and his heart was not in it any more. What else could we do to make a living that we would also enjoy? We talked about simplifying and downsizing our lives: having a smaller house, getting rid of all the animals (eventually chickens, goats, pigs, seven dogs, four birds, and a lizard). Maybe I could get a full time job somewhere and Jeff could be with the kids. During this thought process we remembered a dream of running our own lodge or hotel. We had visited a lodge that was run by a couple on a lake in Colorado and we loved it there, a small place with five self-contained units. So we began looking for a place where Jeff and Wyatt, who love to fish, might also work as fishing guides. We looked at businesses for sale with individual units or an RV camp with water nearby.

We started with Colorado but places there were just too expensive for us. We broadened our search to Utah, Montana, Oregon, and Washington and had maps posted all over our living room wall. There was so much to consider. We needed a safe community for our children and to be near services for Sydney. Her seizures grew worse in the summer heat of New Mexico and we wanted a cooler place to live.

After months of searching on the internet every day we came across a place in Washington state that sounded ideal. It had eleven cottages on the Long Beach peninsula near the Columbia River between the Pacific Ocean and Willapa Bay. Jeff and I flew into Portland for three days and a realtor showed us several possibilities. We considered a couple of bed and breakfast places but quickly decided that wasn't what we wanted. We stayed at Shakti Cove, the property that had caught our imagination, just to get a feel for the place and we loved it. It was a pretty overwhelming trip, though; such a big decision and too little time to go through all the nooks and crannies.

We went home not sure if this place was really right for us. I prayed about it and we waited to see if there were other good options. It was such a huge life change to consider, although it's what we wanted. For eight months more we did online research to check out quality of life issues and potential worries like natural disasters. Sydney was finally comfortable in school and we were worried that such a large change could disrupt her accustomed patterns. At her eighth grade graduation Jeff expressed this concern to her principal who assured us that "Sydney will adjust anywhere you go. Don't let that stop you from doing something that would make you happy. It sounds wonderful and very good for Sydney." Her words helped us feel better with the decision that we were making, and it was about then that we started feeling, "OK. Let's do this!" We were both excited and nervous, and in the end it just came down to a decision for a new life direction. We took the risk, got a loan, made an offer, negotiated, and in August of 2015 Shakti Cove Cottages became our new home. We were charging into the unknown.

I had already been preparing for a change. We had known for a year or so that we wanted a new life so I started going through our accumulated possessions, selling or giving away whatever we didn't need any longer and wouldn't take with us. I began packing early, too. It was a lot of work and in some ways overwhelming at first. Looking back at it now I don't quite know how I managed it all. I decided I would just do one room at a time and I started with our spare storage and art room. Jeff and Wyatt helped with the heavy lifting and repaired things that needed fixing but I did most of the packing myself.

In August we had two weeks left before we needed to move into our new home and start running the cottages. Thank goodness we had kept our first house as a rental property, and with help from family we moved all the boxes into the garage over there so we could get our home ready for sale. Then the moving truck arrived and we had three days to pack it. When we were done there was no empty space left in it at all.

Finally we were packed up and ready to start our long road trip. Wyatt and a cousin drove one car packed to the ceiling; I drove the other with Sydney, her lizard, and everything that we would need for three days on the road. Jeff and his mom drove the truck pulling our four-wheeler and our boat also packed full. We felt exhausted but made it there without any flat tires, mechanical or emotional breakdowns.

No one but Jeff and I had seen our new home. We hoped that the kids would be excited, but mostly they looked tired. We slept in two of the cottages for a few days because the manager was going through the same process of moving out of a house she had occupied for years. She gave Jeff and me some training and soon we were running our new business. Fortunately there were only two cottages rented at the time, which allowed us to get on our feet. Our very first customers that week were understanding, talkative, and excited for us in our new venture. Jeff's mom Carole was so helpful in watching Sydney as we were getting started and her sister, our Aunt Sue, came to help us move into the house. We unpacked the truck, put some things into storage and brought the rest of the boxes into the house where Sue and Carole unpacked them finding a home for everything and fixing up a room for Sydney. The house is much smaller with only two bedrooms, so we set up a curtained area of the living room for Wyatt. After two weeks of training I started cleaning the cottages and doing the laundry on my own. I had always hated doing laundry before, but now that the laundry room is my office I am enjoying it.

Business was still slow, but I was already so busy that I worried about Sydney who was accustomed to living in the country and having a full-time mom. She had to stay in the house and learn a new set of safety rules but she adjusted well. In fact she has really grown up since we moved. She likes her new school and teacher in a class for medically fragile children. At fourteen she is just in a new space of her life that is really working for her and she is gradually becoming more independent.

We have also seen the benefits of a small town school with Wyatt. Though we had lived in the country in New Mexico our children were bussed into more urban schools where they wound up isolated in special education classes. In Ocean Park Wyatt was placed in regular classrooms and not separated from other students, and the schools here give us the sense that they really want the kids to succeed, preparing them to figure out what they want to do in life. As part of their education they do volunteer work and some job shadowing, learning to write essays and resumes that become a portfolio when applying for colleges or jobs. Nevertheless in his junior year Wyatt started getting bored and acting up again to get negative attention. We were so tired of literally fighting with him to get his education, and the school worked with us to consider options that could work for him. He opted to get assignments to do at home, take tests, and meet with his teacher every other week. I still have to remind him to do his schoolwork, though, and I just hope he will make good decisions and earn his high school diploma. He's a hard worker and has become a very caring young man. He has learned from his struggles and that is the most important thing to me. We all have our struggles and challenges, and it is what you do with them that matters.

We had saved up enough to make it through our first year expenses without income, but even in a normally slow season business has been good. Many people who have stayed here over the years continue to come back and we are meeting new people every week. We're still learning, of course, and I really enjoy getting up in the morning to work in our own place. We are settling in, meeting our neighbors, making friends, finding stores and doctors, and becoming part of the Ocean Park community. It has been a huge change but I think it was the best decision we've made and it has already had a large positive impact on all of us.

Moving has required me to grow as a woman as well. Jeff has had to make seasonal trips back to Albuquerque to train the new owner of the landscaping business, and I've found that while he's away I'm capable of running the place myself. For seventeen years I was a stay-at-home mom for our two children with disabilities. Now I am working to support my family and it really makes me feel good. I find I have a smile on my face when I pay for lunch and know how hard I have worked to earn that money. We have been able to hire two part time housekeepers but I still work from the time I get up until it's time to go to bed. Jeff and I are enjoying a pretty good routine of working together. I'm happy to see Jeff not so worn down by physical labor, and we still find time to walk on the beach together.

I also find myself growing closer to God. I have prayed for my family and for wisdom in raising our children, and my prayers are always answered in some way, helping us find peace and get through the hard times. If you had asked me a year ago whether I believed in God I would probably have told you that I believed in a higher power, and also that I had worked too hard in my life to give anyone else the credit for my accomplishments. Man, was I naïve! Now after 40 I understand some things that I wish I had realized when I was younger. I talk to God almost every day now, knowing that God won't judge me and actually just listens without saying anything. God gives me such a peaceful and happy heart that I can handle whatever comes my way even if it is a learning challenge.

I don't begin to understand God's plan for my life or why I had to go through all that I did, but now I know that I am someone, that God loves me, and that I am doing something worthwhile. I love being a mom and that will never change. Parenting is for good and I will always have our kids in my life no matter what their challenges are or who they become. I enjoy having people come visit us and making new friends every day. I appreciate living more simply and having love and peace in my heart. How good life is!

Made in the USA
San Bernardino, CA
09 November 2016